RIDING THE UNIT
SELECTED NONFICTION 1994-2004

mark spitzer

6GP

ISBN-10: 0978296109
ISBN-13: 978-0978296100

Six Gallery Press
P.O. Box 90145
Pittsburgh, PA 15224

Email: editors@sixgallerypress.com

book design by ryan bernhardt at
moustache/moustache
ryan.bernhardt@gmail.com

ACKNOWLEDGMENTS

Versions of these works have appeared in *Thus Spake the Corpse, Vol. 2* (Black Sparrow Press, 2000), *Exquisite Corpse* (the print version), *Minnesota Monthly, RiversEdge, Kinesis, The Southwestern Review, Clackamas Literary Review, Poetic Inhalation, Big Bridge, Jack Magazine* and *The Yale Anglers' Journal.*

I'd like to thank the following humans: George Whitman for the flapjacks; Pete Sniegowski, Melinda McKinnis, Nina de Gramont and Luis & Cindy Urrea for asylum; Kane X. Faucher for the hook-up; Che Elias for going to town; Ryan Bernhardt for cover graphics and layout; Robin Becker for rolling eyeballs (rather than me out the door) and for her invaluable editing; everybody else for everything else; and Kris Hansen — in memoriam of riding the unit together.

—Mark Spitzer
Kirksville, MO
2006.

TABLE OF CONTENTS

DINNER WITH SLINGER

Back in Poetry School, I didn't give a rat's ass about Ed Dorn and he didn't give a shit about me — because in his Literature of the High Plains class I was the guy who sat in the farthest corner, stoned outta my gourd, writing poetry and not paying any attention to him. And why should I? I mean, the class was the Ed Dorn Show: Each week he'd get up there and shout about different atrocities — and to pay attention to this was to embellish an ego the size of Charles Olson.

So it went on like this for months: Col. Wingnut and Gruff Dave coming on over to my subterranean earwig-hole which Kowalski and I rented up on 4th Street — and then we'd all do bongs and eat a herd of "free rangers" (which is what we called potatoes — and margarine was "sauce") — and then we'd make a stop at Liquor Mart and get some beer and go to class.

In which the highlight happened mid-way through the semester when we found ourselves sitting there and Dorn raging back and forth, ranting that if somebody thinks he doesn't have a teaching method, and if that somebody wants a professor with a teaching method, then that somebody should get the hell out of his class and go take a class from some nun!

Then Dorn (obviously drunk) went on, howling about how he doesn't drink, and how he doesn't do drugs, and blah

blah blah (the windbag), until finally Gruff Dave (after 45 minutes) jumped in and said "Excuse me, Ed... what are you talking about?"

To which Dorn replied "What am I talking about!? What am I talking about!? I'll tell you what I'm talking about! I'm talking about an individual here who lodged a complaint against me! As if the Chair cares! I mean, the Chair's a friend of mine! I see him in the hallway! He comes up to me and says 'I know you didn't do it, Ed,' and I say 'Yeah, I know!'"

Then Dorn ranted for another hour — but before he even got that far, he managed to drive the accuser forth: The guy was in his early 40s, balding, and wearing a gay white suit — and he got up, walked out, left the classroom, the class, and never came back.

But wait! There are more anecdotes, and the first one has to do with squawfish — a subject I did a project on in his class, because thanks to "horsepower" they're an endangered species now, their upstream runs are dammed, and the Navajos don't give a damn — because concrete means jobs and Camaros with V8s and "home entertainment centers."

Anyhow, there was a drunken discussion in Dorn's kitchen at the end-of-the-year class party where I found myself outright lying to Dorn (a notorious promoter of "the outrageous statement" anyway), telling him that squawfish swim a hundred miles to lay their eggs, that the males guard the young, and that with the full moon squawfish rise at night to croon their noodling fish tunes. And Dorn was nodding impatiently back, because he's an expert on the West and this is common information — which is something I'd know if I read more Brautigan or Edward Abbey!

And another thing: Back in 1990 when I first came to Poetry School, I didn't know anybody and I was at a party

2

for new grad students and that's when I met Dorn all craggy faced and slugging on a bottle of Jim — and not too long after that he started in lecturing me about how the Brazilians are coming up to the Dakotas abducting children, then taking them down to South America to stick in the deep freeze for body parts.

And as Dorn raved on, I noticed that he wasn't really speaking to me — he was speaking to the booze, the wall, nobody — just shooting off his mouth with all the indifference of some crabby old granddad barking at the six o'clock news and not expecting any response. Plus, it was also apparent that both of us would rather be talking to somebody a bit more nubile.

But then there's something I'm not supposed to talk about — since I promised Mona Groan (my girlfriend at the time in an on/off, on/off relationship based on sex and petty judgments) I'd never reveal what she confided in me — having to do with the infamous Christmas party when Dorn got all drunk and cornered her and told her "Ya know what I'd like to do? I'd like to stick my tongue in your pussy!"

To which Mona, incensed, objected "Don't you know who my father is!?" (another prof in the English Department) But Dorn didn't care — he grabbed her instead, shoved her up against the wall, stuck his tongue way down her throat, and squeezed her boobs with all the grace of a rapist.

So yesterday, me and Extreme are cruising down to Denver for a dinner Dorn's throwing for students who defended their theses — and I'm looking forward to talking to Dorn because he's Dorn — and if he was me and I was him, he should talk to me, so I should talk to him — and when we get there the place is full of studii and profs and food and booze — and Dorn recognizes me but can't tell me from the

3

3000 generic others he's had the pleasure of hating over the last how-ever-many years — and then I see an Ezra Pound CD sitting there. So thinking back to Hemingway's *Feast*, I figure here's a good place to start a conversation up — so totally blunder, asking Dorn "Isn't Pound supposedly the ugliest poet ever?" then quick, I remember it was Wyndham Lewis, so amend the question.

And Dorn — à la baseball hat, erosion-face and Don Johnson-looking with his t-shirt under blazer — says "Number one, Wyndham Lewis wasn't a poet! And number two, Ezra Pound was known for being quite dashing!"

And he just keeps going, attacking and attacking, smashing the bones of my stupid statement into a mush while I stand there thinking: *Theoretically, I should be enjoying this — and hypothetically, I should be valuing this — cuz I'm talking to such a historical guy, who is in effect shrinking me just for the sake of shrinking me so he becomes a giant...*

Till I realize something I forgot: If you ain't a nudie gal beneath your clothes, then when it comes to this arrogant blowhard, Communication = Antagonism.

I turn him off and wander outside, thinking that whenever I consider going back to school, it's dynamics like this which make me see the lameness, and thus the conclusion: "Fuck em all... just write!"

So I'm standing there in Dorn's backyard talking to Peter Michelson (who I modeled the Grizzly Professor on in a big fish story, and used to feel intimidated by — like the time all liquored up at Matt Cooperman's when Peter told me "Spitzer you asshole, you can't get to Iowa City on a river!") (though mostly it's his towering presence and the fact that he's so calculated and intellectual and I'm just the opposite: spur-of-the-moment and absurd) — but now that we don't have

4

to deal with each other, my tension's gone away — so we start
talking about Lorna's house — because Lorna, who's a big-
time Chicana poet and ten years older than me and already
part of the modern canon (meaning she's in the *Norton*), got
an NEA and went to Mexico, leaving her place with the Griz
— and then Daddy-O (who just sold two big books to two
big publishers) came on up from San Diego to rent the joint
— and when he got there the place was soaked in cat piss
and dog piss (and maybe even human piss) and the electricity
was cut off and no heat and no phone — so Daddy-O was
ticked and telling everyone this drama — and then he asked
me if I wanted to live in "the shit-hole," so I said "Yeah" and
spent a week scrubbing the place and even yanked the carpet
— which is what Peter and I are yucking about.

Because when I first took a class from Lorna, we (the
students) were sitting around in that very house and had to
address the question "Have you ever had to scrub somebody
else's toilet before?" Because it was one of those confessional-
type workshops in which victims become empowered by
digging up dirt — so by the end of the semester, as it turns
out, everybody in the class except for me admits to being
raped.

Then Peter and I look over at the back steps, where
it's *The Ed Dorn Show* again — and he's got an audience
gathered all around him and he's wavering as he tries to pull
himself up the stairs — but the hand rail is elusive and Dorn
is stumbling, falling up, shouting (whoknowswhy?) "Pollacks!
Pollacks! Give Me A Hundred Thousand Pollacks!"

And a few drinks later, inside, he's sitting at the table
with a bunch of brown-nose groupies gathered all around him,
laughing at his jokes, agreeing with his blurtings, applauding
him on — and he's eating chicken *mole* and ranting that he's

5

an expatriate in his own country and should've been born in Europe, so therefore he's gonna sue — to which someone responds "Who ya gonna sue, Ed? Your parents? The government?"

"HELL NO!" Dorn exclaims. "I'll sue the Indians! It's their country isn't it!? I'll sue the Arapahoes! That's what I'll do!"

I decide to sit and listen to his wisdom.

"Hey! Is that whiskey!?" Dorn demands. "Screw this wine shit!"

Then we're sitting there with a bottle of Johnny between us and he's telling me about how his new house is bullshit: 200 feet this direction, 500 feet that direction — owned by some shifty East Coast bank investing in the hypodermics sucking dry the Ecuadorian rainforest "which has more species in its one jungle than the rest of the planet even knows exist!" — and how us stupid-ass Americans are bleeding that country for the equivalent of thirteen days use of fuel thanks to "George Bush and his mutant son who ripped off Denver and fled!"

Dorn then goes on to inform me that "There should be no cars! No cars, no planes, no trains, just horses! Hell, every day I walk five miles to visit a friend!"

"Haw!" I laugh, right in his face — as Extreme, behind me, yells out:

"That's a load a crap, Ed!"

And Dorn stares his disappointment into me (as if I, like everybody, am supposed to believe his myth of the moment, then take it and repeat it for the sake of his legend) and "What!?" he explodes. "You're saying I don't have any friends?"

"No," I shoot back, "I just don't believe you're that

6

honorable, Ed!"

"Bomb the Chinese!" Dorn replies. "That's what we gotta do! Bomb the Chinese! There's a war coming up! A big war!"

Which leads to the Apocalypse (a discussion of), Dorn claiming that Eliot's whimper will be an exaggeration.

"What whimper?" I ask — and Dorn slaps his forehead in disbelief. Because I don't know nothing. Because I'm just some dumb guy, another anonymous member of the decade.

"Where the hell do you go to school!?" Dorn demands.

"University of Colorado," I tell him. "Went."

"You taught him, Ed!" Extreme says.

"Jesus Christ!" Dorn goes on. "The whimper! It's only the most famous line in all of literature since 'To be or not to be!'"

"Hmmmmm," Extreme ponders, reaching for some bourbon, "isn't it something like 'the world won't end with a bang, but rather in a whimper'?"

But Dorn doesn't answer, because two giggly grad-gals walk on in with shapely calves — so Dorn pays attention to them (his eyes lit with orgy scenes) — till eventually Extreme and I say later date and take off to buy some pot.

And as we're driving, I hear myself say "Ya know, Dorn's wrong. There will be a whimper, even if it's a monotonous three-century whimper. I mean, what the hell is he talking about? If he's a guy who speaks for some sorta disenfranchised generation, then his voice is a whimper. I mean, that's what he does. He whimpers for those who don't."

"I dunno," Extreme says. "Why even try?"

"But," I counter, "what he's talking about — it's like

7

the whimper of a collective historical consciousness. It's like he's saying there will be less than a whimper because the world's so fractioned, and the media's been dulling us, cuz individuals are so involved in their own stupid things — like dumb fuzzy dice dangling from our rear-view mirrors and all the crap that we feed on and capitalize on instead of what we used to do, which is read more and appreciate art more, which is intelligence supposedly — "

"I wonder who the Poet of our Generation will be," Extreme interrupts.

And me: "That's what I'm talking about. There won't be a Poet of Our Generation, because people stopped caring about that thirty years back, thanks to t.v. and gasoline — which is the focus of our consciousness now, if anything — which is why the Poet of Any Generation doesn't exist ANYMORE and isn't a concern — which is why Frank O'Haras don't count and the game's over!"

"Man," Extreme says, "we were raised on corporate shit... suckled on nothing."

"Yeah," I agree. "But there will be a whimper, because even a little population, like say 300 people — when they get wiped out, there's a whimper — cuz ya can't measure how big a minimum whimper is."

"Awwww, quit yer whining," Extreme tells me — and we get off at Colfax, stop at a cash machine, punch some buttons, and receive $120 for an ounce of shwagg.

"Damn," Extreme says, "we suck."

"Yeah," I say, "let's go get fucked up."

DINNER AT MY MOTHER'S

When I come home from smashing concrete (WHAM!
WHAM! WHAM! whamming in my head) my mother is
sitting on the couch, reading that Berryman book I gave
her (which she originally gave to me) and "Mark," she says
(trying to get me to look in her eyes, but I won't), "don't grow
up to be a crazy poet, okay?"

But I don't answer. I just use the silence, letting it
hang there — until she (my silver-haired mother — to make a
stereotype) tells me:

"So... I started reading this book today. And it's
upsetting, because... well, here I am... and there you are... and
there he is with all his eccentricities and self-absorptions, and
well... do you know what I'm trying to get at? It's as if there's
a pattern that all these crazy poets fall into: drugs, alcohol,
thinking society is ignoring them... and, well, you do know,
don't you... you don't have to be a crazy poet..."

"I know that," I snap. "But it's not like there's some
sorta Crazy Poet's Club. Those guys didn't do what they did
to be like each other. They were young and brilliant. They
were white guys. They had conflicts just like everyone. But
since they were writers, they were whining about it — and
that's what's tragic. Even more tragic than their actual fall.
Some people can't deal. Others can. You only read about the

9

whiners."

"Well then," my mother says, her voice getting chokier, "Warren's upstairs eating cheese and crackers. He's watching Henry the Fifth."

* * *

I go up and watch with him.

Warren is my stepfather. He's a big deal American potter. The Japanese make movies about him. People write books about him. He hates the attention — the power of his name. We eat cheese and crackers.

There are three kinds of cheese. Yellow cheese, orange cheese, and brown cheese. The brown cheese is a goaty cheese.

On TV:

The guy says the thing about his horse being his mistress and the King sneaks out of camp, meets up with the peasant kid, and the peasant kid makes a great pre-battle speech:

"If all the bones and bodies should rise wailing for their heads, looking for surgeons, then something something something something..." Then the clincher: "If a whole lotta men give their souls for the King, and if the King doesn't something-or-other, then that's a black matter for the King."

Then some more scenes. Horses. Music.

* * *

Dinner: We eat sweet corn. Always in the summer, we eat sweet corn — while Warren and I get into another typical big old argument, this time on Shakespeare.

10

I say there's an intentional homo-eroticism going on in the movie. I say that when the King lowers his hand slowly, the scene is designed to appear as if he's stroking the head of the sleeping kid. It's a gesture, I explain.

"Bullshit," Warren says.

I argue that the King transfers his affection for the kid to the knight whom he touches in the next scene — because when the knight walks in to fetch the King, the King says real real slow and dramatic-like "Good knight."

"Bullshit," Warren says.

Warren says "I think this is another case of a critic reading more into a work than the artist ever intended. I'd hate it if somebody looked at my pots and tried to tell me what I thought."

I tell Warren he's reacting to psychoanalysis, not my point. I tell him about *Hamlet* — the old movie — how the camera focuses at the stars and the vastness out in space, then zooms on into act III, panning down to the Prince of Denmark sitting on a high-up rock above the sea — until eventually the descending camera is focusing right on his cranium, right on his balding spot, which is shaped like a galaxy — and then the camera starts zooming into it, turning and turning — and that's when *Hamlet* says "To be or not to be..."

"Therefore," I argue, "every single scene in every single one of those movies was totally planned out, because there's never just one message, there's always a few being delivered."

Warren, however, just shakes his head.

"Gestures!" I implore, gripping my corn. "Intentional gestures! Not just empty gestures!"

"Eat your cucumber salad," my mother tells me.

11

* * *

Then I see a woodchuck sitting on a boulder out in the yard.

Woodchucks get into the garden. Woodchucks destroy.

So "A woodchuck," I say, "sitting on a boulder in the yard."

And Warren says "Where!?"

"There," I say, pointing out the window.

Warren jumps up, runs to the door, opens it and yells "Get outta here, you fucker!"

The woodchuck runs away. I laugh.

I laugh because Warren is 70-something years old and he's standing there with his white beard and jaw thrust out and his fists clenched up and he's breathing hard and shaking like an oldporchman.

An oldporchman is a retired guy who spends his time hating squirrels, so waits — watching a stainless steel rat trap — for some squirrel to come along and set a paw on his lawn. An oldporchman is also fond of phrases like "CUT OUT THE GRAB-ASS!" and "GIT OFFA MY LAWN, YOU DAMN KIDS!" And if a whiffle ball ever lands on an oldporchman's lawn, that whiffle ball is gone forever.

I laugh again. Warren called the woodchuck a fucker. He threatened it.

Then Warren goes into his woodchuck story, which my mother and I have heard at least a hundred times. This time, however, I don't listen to his tale of heading down to the pottery and running into an oversized bristle-naped woodchuck hissing in the path — and how it refused to budge, even when he hurled some dirt clods at it. Because this time,

12

I'm planning my response.

"Warren," I tell him when he finishes, "I noticed this in your pottery too. You feel a deep menace from woodchucks."

"Grrrrrr!" Warren grumbles.

* * *

My mother sits back down on the couch, opens up the Berryman book.

"I'm curious," she says, "you made a couple of notes in this book. Can I discuss them with you?"

"I guess so."

"Well, the first one was a correction in grammar, which I agree with, but the second one had to do with something about suicide."

"Maw, I ain't gonna ice myself. I got too many projects going on for that. I wouldn't get anything done."

"Well, I just want to know what's going on in your head. There are things I was hoping we could discuss, like approaches in our art that we both take, and what we're really trying to say."

I don't say anything. It doesn't interest me to talk about this.

Silence again.

Then after a bit:

"It's just so disturbing," she says, staring through the book on her lap. "I mean, we all know what happens in the end... he jumps off the bridge. Still, I continue reading, hoping he'll change. It's frustrating."

I shrug, sit down, write this. It's still not close enough to the truth.

13

ON THE RIVER WITH MY FATHER

So we're motoring up the Mississippi River, my dad in the back, running the two-stroke, and me up front, feet propped up, cutting along steadily — when I remember his vision ain't that hot.

My father steers too close to deadheads, riversnags, sandbars — and when the wake of another boat comes our way, I see it forty feet before he even knows it's there, a threat to the canoe. So I tense all up, wondering if he'll hit it. It's always a few feet before he sees it and veers away.

I find myself staring upstream. Basically, I see two points. The first is as far as I can see, the second is half-way in between. I squint, the river blurs. Now I can't see any herons.

"Look," my father says, as if we haven't passed twenty already, "a blue heron."

Meanwhile, there are soft-shelled turtles up and down the muddy banks, lounging in the sunrays. And on one of these shores we stop for lunch. Ham and cheese, mustard on bread.

"Can you see the turtles?" I ask him.

"What turtles?" he asks back.

I point them out.

There are seven turtles on a nearby island. Two are the size of manhole covers. They've been sliding in and out of these murkwaters for decades, maybe even a century.

"Hmmmmm," my father squints, sighting down the line I draw in the air. "Hmmmmm... hmmmmm..." He still can't see them.

"Four o' clock," I tell him, "from the branch, three feet from shore."

"Hmmmmm... hmmmmm..."

I point out turtles, I point out minnows, I point out all the creatures he can't see. I want him to see what I can see. I paint the color of their backsides, the directions of their frontsides. He nods, peering harder, and it becomes more important for me than I ever figured to point out what he's missing.

"Hmmmmm... hmmmmmm..."

Then, on the opposite island, I notice activity. There are screeching herons circling the spires: nine or ten or twelve of them, taking off and landing. It's a rookery. I can see their nests, their long gray necks protruding. So I point them out and count them out loud. But he can't see a single one.

"Maybe your imagination," he suggests, "is seeing more than your eyes."

I stop counting.

* * *

"Talked to Rachel's mother last night," my father tells me, cig clenched between his teeth, talking out the side of his mouth. "She was pretty relieved about Rachel. Seems she left that... *person* she was with."

"Yeah," I say, "Fucking Ava. That's what I heard too. Good for Rachel. Fucking Ava was just as ugly on the outside as she felt on the inside... projecting all that bile."

"Fucking Ava!" my father laughs. "I met her down at Powderhorn once. Couldn't stand her. Nobody could. I think everyone's a little relieved now."

And then his voice starts to change. It's like he's searching his innerhead or something.

"Rachel," he tells me, in a tone I immediately recognize as that tone I hate, "she had a lovely body... a lot like your grandmother's... when your grandmother was her age."

But I refuse to play this game. He's pushing it again. My gramma is his mother and I'm not gonna sit and squirm with the thoughts he's trying to stick in my head. He can have those for himself.

I clench my jaw. Turn him off. He stares at herons he can't see.

* * *

Now we're motoring down the river and he's steering too close to other boats.

At one point, he pulls up right next to a canoe. Gets five or six feet away from it, then smiles at the guys and waves while I refuse to meet their gaze.

People on the river, especially in canoes, want to be left alone.

And every time he sees a boat (be it conscious or not) he swings their way. Even if that boat is ten times bigger than us, he'll start making for it — and then, as always, they'll change their course and head away.

So it goes on like this for miles and miles: My father bullying boats away and me not saying anything — just kicking back in the bow, wondering if he's doing this on purpose or if he's just oblivious — and is this hereditary?

17

All of the above, I decide.

He's been this way so long it's automatic now.

But I don't dwell on it. Instead, beat from sun and beer and a couple puffs out there on the island, I drift away in the motor's drone, the chime-like rocking of the hull.

And there, in the all-consuming blare, with the hum of a distant highway rising, I find balance in the bow.

Closing my eyes, I shut off the smokestacks, the power plants, NSP. Limbo grips me.

* * *

JERK! I jerk awake — and I know my father sees me do it. But he can't feel what's in my heart. It's pounding like a motherfucker.

It was the engine... blaring. It was the noise... rising, diving. It was the up/down up/down Evinrude rhythm.

And in that rhythm, in those vibrations, I thought I heard a rumble. A growing growling comingatchya rumble. It was unidentifiable and manifesting. And then I knew: It was the Roar of the Apocalypse. A nuclear windstorm was searing its way across the planet, incinerating the prairies, the cities, everything. It was upon us. I jerked awake.

Last time I jerked like that was on the train to Morocco. I never wanted to go to Morocco. Never even thought of it. But she was the most flipped-out little weirdo I had ever met, and she had a sock full of money and took me on a journey and I fell asleep with my head on her lap. And in that darkness I started falling. So jerked in the Nothing. And she caught me. That was the danger.

It was a completely deranged experience. I wanted to believe stuff that just wasn't real. I wanted to believe it so much that I made myself see things that didn't exist. And hear things and feel things that never were. My imagination was out of control. But that was the way I wanted it.

She told me things that were totally wiggy. Like how me and three guys had come to Paris to hook up because of this thing called the Thing — which would change the world.

And I believed her — because of the stuff that was happening around us: stuff so unreal it had to be real. Like Chinese ghosts trying to get us, and telepathic plague victims channeling archaic verse, and dancing lights and stuff like that. Because we were willing to let the fantastic consume us.

It was determined that my role was that of *The Eyeball*, and that my job was to oversee the construction of the Thing. Whatta load of crap that was!

And then she burned me. It was expected. Though I can't really say she did it by herself. I mean, if I never would've believed all that stuff to the degree I did, I never would've had the incredible romantic brainwashed adventure that — in part — made me who I am.

But then again, maybe I didn't believe all that stuff. Maybe I was only playing along to the point where the story distorted the world — because what could be better than creating yourself into a character, then plotting the course of that character's life instead of a bunch of circumstances doing it for you like everyone else?

So I wrote a novel all about it. And I wrote it so much and repeated it so much that whatever truth there was in it got lost in the rush. Until the story became the only truth.

But that's what happens when delusions take over. A guy can be right, even if he's wrong. Then looking back, he can see where he screwed up and use that failure to his advantage.

19

Because something sticks with you. Something that tells you there's a way you should be — despite knowing you've deceived yourself and can't even trust yourself. And it has little to do with what's logical. And it's the hardest thing in the world to shake.

* * *

My father forces a pontoon Winnebago to turn toward shore and his engine keeps on droning.

Lately, I've been thinking Africa... Rwanda... Zaire. The other day, the paper said there's 100,000 children out wandering the terra — and today on the news: cholera — thousands in the dirt, laid out on mats, holding bloating bellies — moaning, puking, bloody in the mud — dying so fast they can't be counted. No doubt, there's a death stench in the air.

And here I am, running around with a bong in one hand and a hard-on in the other, embellishing the adventures of a clean white kid who runs around for the sheer sake of running around, getting in and out of trouble, meeting whacky characters and being idealistic — and that's about it.

Me: I don't know no horror. All I know is the fear of it. If I am *The Eyeball*, I should point at death, I should point at disease, I should point at war, environment, genocide. I should be good. And do as much as I can.

Yeah, I figure, *I'll be P.C.!*

SPLASHHH!

Water hits my shoulder, my neck, the back of my head — like a sign from some god I don't believe in telling me to shut the fuck up.

We're passing beneath a walking bridge. I look up. There's a kid in a wheelchair up there. He's hydrocephalic, limbs all twisted — and in a hand that's just a stub, he's holding a plastic bottle. His cheeks are filled with water and he's waiting for my father to pass beneath him.

"FUCK YOU!" his expression tells me. "FUCK YOU, YOU BAG OF FUCKING SHIT!"

No shit: He's challenging me, daring me, taunting me to come up there and knock him over — then stand above his crippled frame and laugh at him while he laughs at me, sneering a white-hot sneer at me — hating me — wanting to kill me with all the strength left in his withered body.

But what can you do, what can you say?

I don't try to figure it out.

Like most people, I turn away.

DEMISE OF THE BOOKSTORE HISTORY

"Have You Ever!?" George Whitman demanded. "Ever!?
Published A Word Of Nonfiction In Your Life!?"

"Sure," I answered.

And the next thing I knew, my new title was Store
Historian.

It only lasted a couple of weeks.

* * * * *

SUNDAY SEPT 18, 1994, PARIS: another autumn
Sunday tea party up in George Whitman's fourth-story
apartment overlooking the Seine: publishers and editors,
poets and expatriates, raincoats and biscuits — served by
Majella and Steph, our hostesses this afternoon. They're
Australian and dwelling here at Shakespeare — like me.

Then WHAM: George bursts in. He takes big strides,
shakes hands like a madman, then disappears at mach speed
before his voice can even leave the room.

George is the owner of this bookstore. He's been
described as *whacky, eccentric, a character,* and other words
which are only words, so leave many things out.

But back to the bookstore — where, down below,

23

tourists and bibliophiles and students and drifters browse amidst the bindings, then wander up to the Sylvia Beach Library, asking questions all the time. Which rise like helium to George's uppermost apartment — where a certain individual has just furtively raised some chit-chat to ponder.

Translation: "What exactly is this place?"

The answers vary:

"Somewhere where Literature exists in the instant," a freshly pressed overcoat replies.

"A place where the past survives despite the future," a mustache informs us.

"Perhaps," an immaculate umbrella breaks in, "a history of the events which unfurl here, as they unfurl here, can better detail what goes on here."

Then, from the corner, an obstinate typewriter (previously warned to keep its clatter to itself) bursts out:

"*History* is the French word for *story*!"

This outburst is ignored by all and the tea party continues.

* * * * *

MONDAY SEPT 19, 1994: There are two cats here: Kitty and Jackal. Kitty, the yellow cat with the spiraling pattern, is the senior feline. Jackal is the white cat. Today Jackal stepped in blue ink, then walked on Céline and Kerouac.

* * * * *

TUESDAY SEPT 20, 1994: two new residents today: a woman from Malaysia and another from Singapore.

George detected them from up above, forelorn and sad-faced, hunching under backpacks, and was instantly aware of their desperate situation: They, for some unjust reason, had just been kicked out of the Hotel Esmerelda. And so George, acting swiftly, mobilized the entire Shakespeare and Company crew, employees as well as residents — and a few expatriates, not to mention a handful of customers — and en masse, we went streaming into the streets chanting "BE NOT INHOSPITABLE TO STRANGERS/LEST THEY BE ANGELS IN DISGUISE!!" until we convinced them of George's great concern — and gathering them up, we carried them back on our shoulders with tears of gratitude flooding from their eyes.

Everyone who stays here has a responsibility. Some must read a book per day, others must either sell or stack, open up or close the shop, fix things up, guard the store from biblio-thieves, run errands, or — sometimes — scrub.

Morgan, a jolly and informative technical writer (who was once a friar), has been here almost two years. Soon he will leave for Beijing to open a new Shakespeare and Co — with Pia, who is some sorta goddess, so I hear. It is rumored that she will be the Sylvia Beach of the Orient. I await her ascension into this story — I mean history.

Right now, there is a Panamanian law student named Ariel living here, attending the University of Paris as a doctoral candidate — as well as an American vagapoet earning his keep as the Store Historian.

I've seen this happen before — it doesn't work. First the word "I" appears, and then that person drifts away. The problem with vagapoets is they have no concept of how to be serious. History is a serious thing. Stories ain't.

Stories operate on conflicts.

A literature professor will tell you there are three

major types of conflicts: Man versus Man, Man versus Nature, and Man versus Self. But a Shakespeare Historian will tell you there is only one: Historian versus George.

Thus, the moon continues to orbit the earth, and we all die from either violence or disease, sometimes loving in between.

* * * * *

SERIOUS VOICE: The members of last Sunday's tea party included: Gordon Freeman, radiation chemist from Alberta; Ted Joans, poet/poseur, and his matching female companion, so stylish in their smart hats and smart suits quite consciously coordinated; Alan Rodi and Marian Elizabeth Sherwood, English teachers; M.L. Stein, editor and publisher; Roy Williamson (calls himself an "écrivain"); Daria ("an angel in the sky," so she claims); Jill Freeman ("blown by the mistrals," and who knows what else?); A. Kressner, retired interpreter; Chris Correale from South Korea; Marian Cunningham (not from *Happy Days*); Thomas Goullet de Rxxxxx, art student; and of course, the Overcoat, the Mustache, the Umbrella and the Typewriter.

* * * * *

WEDNESDAY SEPT 21, 1994: A new guy is here: Mikkel from Denmark. He has come in search of the music scene.

The Henry Miller Society also met. It was reported that George spoke about lepers today.

Elephantiasis is not leprosy!

* * * * *

A BIT ON THE HISTORY OF THE
NEIGHBORHOOD: George is standing in the Paris dusk,
once again sporting his faded maroon corduroy suit, thinking
thoughts which could change the world — but he keeps them
to himself. The world will have to get by without any guidance
from him this time. I approach him.

"So George, anything historical happen today?"

"Yes, yes," he says, grabbing me by the shoulder
and pointing up the street, "you see that guy, that guy in the
black suit? Well, he's the son of the man, the man I gave the
roundtrip ticket to... from Paris to New York, because I gave
away eight free trips, you see... flew eight people, flew them
from Boston to Paris... a scholarship, yes it was a scholarship,
to live here and write here, to write... a writing scholarship for
three months! And that guy there, he's the son of the man
— yes, he got himself a room in this building right around
the corner there — NO NO NO, not there, THERE! And that
man, he's a big man, fell down, fell down right here, right
here... so I helped him up, carried him over here, carried
him! But now he's in the hospital over there... tubes! Has
tubes in him, going in and out of him, he was bleeding from
the rectum, terrible terrible mess... oil family, though, made it
really big in Peking. Big tycoon... put that down, you can put
that down can't you?"

"Even the part about the bloody rectum?"

"Yes, yes. All the details, why not!? There was
blood all over the toilet. Toilet full of blood! That's his
son over there. Eight round trips. Put that down too, put
it under the heading: A BIT ON THE HISTORY OF THE
NEIGHBORHOOD!"

27

So "Okay, George," I say, and climb the red steps to the tangerine typer, sit down and take a glug.

Morgan, also, is drinking redwine.

* * * * *

FRIDAY SEPT 23, 1994: a slight spectacle last night concerning the historical tree growing in front of the shop. An individual, who at one point must've heard George voice his disdain for the tree (since it blocks his view of France and France's view of his store) — this individual appeared after closing time, brandished a saw, and went to work madfully sawing branches off, then dragging them across the street and dumping them in the Seine, laughing hysterically all the while. And as I objectively watched (note: Since I am "the Historian" here, any interference or assistance in this matter would upset the cosmic order of All), a group of five or six concerned men from the café next door appeared and surrounded the tree (in which the individual was raving in the foliage, still sawing away beneath the full moon) — and the men, who apparently objected, demanded to know who granted authority for this — and the individual, he pointed in a direction somewhere beyond the rue de la Bûcherie, then leapt down, gathered up the limbs he cut, and went running toward the river, where he vanished like the night into the night.

Instantly, a posse was formed of twenty men connected with the café and a van full of gendarmes with flashlights arrived. The area was scoured, but they couldn't find the mysterious culprit. It was only after they all gave up and left that he reappeared, came walking up to me, and stood before me grinning like a lunatic — who, no doubt, after planning and pondering the architecture of this evening, was now deep in the ecstasy of his adrenalized visions. All I can say about his appearance is that he was tall and curly and blond with a Scottish essence in him, and was once a boy — because there, beneath the lines and creases of what I can only describe as an utter and complete abandon of something once again embellishing its limited time on earth (something that would otherwise keep his expressions solid, rather than volcanically surging with facial tics and tremors beneath the mantle of his maskface), the traces of a mischievous and incorrigible childhood were beaming with release, his quivering visage —

"Tell the old guy," he instructed me, "I'll be back within five nights to finish off the tree!" Then laughing maniacally (like crazed characters in stories), he shot off, stabbing the sky with his saw.

No doubt, he will return.

* * * * *

TUESDAY SEPT 27, 1994: a "surreal weekend," according to the Aussie women (I don't know — was gone in the country for a wedding).

Lisa Stevenson and Merrin McLeod, two New Zealanders robbed in Rome, drifted in and drifted out; as did Julian, a British student at the Sorbonne, who's been staying here for years; and then there was some phantom female searching for an aspirin in the night.

Anne Driscol, a freelance columnist for *The Boston Globe*, was rewarded by George when she discovered his missing keys and brought them to him, thus interrupting his crowbarring/hammering maelstrom in the hallway. George was trying to bust the lock — but when the keys appeared he took out a massive wad of francs (thousands) and threw them at her feet. It was quite a show, so I hear.

That was the day of the massive cleaning binge, when Majella and Steph went scrubbing and grubbing through George's apartment at a manic pace, which continued into the evening — when a jazz band arrived and jazzed it up outside and fireworks burst above the Seine. Then Claude (whoever he is) stole Steph's candy bar.

* * * * *

ON SUNDAY René came around. René can only be described as a greasy pig, due to his lascivious attempts at luring young lambs into his lair, where unspeakable atrocities are hopefully more masturbated about than actually carried out. René is a Frenchman with negative charm, vulture breath, and no redeeming value whatsoever (except, perhaps, that he's willing to pay whomever he molests) — so I won't make any more stereotypes except to say this: To know him is to bleed for the death of Beauty in the face of those who would suck it up and shit it out like a sausage.

René is also a notorious loiterer. And since George doesn't want René in the building, and since repeated attempts to purge him from the premises have failed (because, as centuries have shown us, you can't have *good* without *evil*), impending tea parties become ambiguous when René is around. Thus, much time was spent on Sunday trying to organize the event without alerting the vile swine to its existence. The tea party, therefore, was cut short this time.

Lubermeir, expatriate handyman/familiar-face-at-Shakespeare, was there as well as a few South American women and David Turner, Australian architect; not to mention a·well-known Hindu author of four books by Penguin.

Not much news on the pancake breakfast.

* * * * *

ON MONDAY I knock on George's door to get a key, and there he is in his buttoned-up shirt and Batman cap. He invites me in, sits me down, and drills me for twenty minutes on the tree-trimming incident — then tells me more on what he wants to see in the history:

"More facts, more details, make it interesting... You don't have to exaggerate... just tell the truth... and tell about YOURSELF, what YOU do... what YOUR experiences are... and the girls, the Australian girls too! Tell about the NIGHT LIFE of the residents!"

"Okay George," I tell him, reluctant though obedient, since the risk involved in exaggeration is sometimes as much as its opposite.

* * * * *

THE AUSTRALIAN GALS cook cous-cous and audition for *Dracula*. On Thursday and Sunday nights Majella sings at the bar around the corner (Friar Morgan in the corner). Toward the end of the evening it usually gets pretty whacky. As the Saints come marching in, so do the misfits and Tweedle-dees. The energy rises and so do the octaves. Those with booze in their blood join in. Then we, Shakespearian weirdos, wander back to the store as the Waltzing Matildas bust out the Australian anthem.

Other nights, we wander out to bars, sometimes with Constantin (who works the 8 to 12 shift at "the case") and Roy, who I strike up a conversation with concerning Death — and Death gets Roy jabbering.

(And when those who have the gall to call themselves "poets" start talking Death, vast generalizations get made. And when vast generalizations get made, Roy starts buying rounds on his credit card)

The next thing I know, Constantin's agreeing with me that this is not a regular place. It's all based on deviations and mutations, what's outside the norm, and what should be rather than what is. The thing is, though, not much embellishment is necessary for a historian. The characters were ready-made for me when I arrived. All I do is watch them and write about what they do, for they are the designers of this story (I mean history) — not me.

In a way, writing the history of Shakespeare & Co is a lot like translating the poetry of Jean Genet — which is my main project here. In French, the poems often don't make sense. Sometimes the subject is twelve miles from the verb and adjectives modify air. Secret language permeates. Thus, it's my job to make sense of what doesn't makes sense.

Edmund White is a celebrated American writer in Paris. When it comes to Genet, he wrote the book. George asked me what we had for lunch.

"Canard et calamar," I told him.

"How much did it cost — 300 francs?" George was eager to know.

"I dunno," I responded, "a hundred and something."

"Three-hundred francs!" George shot back. "Put 300 francs down!"

But back to Constantin: He's a shifty little conman who's been working for George for years. Sometimes at night a bottle of redwine appears at the register, and then three or

32

five people partake of the grape and it turns into a party.

Then there's Karl, who usually works 12 to 4. He's an expert on old books and the publisher of Alyscamps Press. Most of his books have to do with Henry Miller.

According to myth, Henry Miller's ghost haunts the bookstore. The real ghoul, however, is a bit more Oriental — but then there's a more compassionate ghost. For more information on these apparitions look for some novel called *Remember the Orange-Glow*. Or something like that. I can't remember the author's name.

* * * * *

ANYWAY, last night the Aussies and I went out with Anne Driscol and ended up in her hotel room near St. Michel with beaujolais and bordeaux. Got buzzed. Talked.

Anne is doing a story on "A Writer's Paris." I put in my two cents: There ain't no passion anymore! The *writers* here, like everywhere else, are all self-serving egotists lacking content, and none of em fighting for Music or Color or the Twist-in-the-Gut!

My main complaint: "There's no movement here. Poetry's dead!" My second main complaint: "Nothing new or innovative or intriguing is being done with language." My third main complaint: "Voice, and the direction of voice, is valued for its trendiness!"

The arguments get abstract, but one thing that's totally clear is my total disgust for the concept of "a writer's Paris" — which drives me into drunkeness. Majella too.

* * * * *

WEDNESDAY the 28th, 1994: There's a new guy
working here: Will from Europe. Will is an art student
working on his master's degree. His jobs vary. He dusts and
scrubs and stacks and stocks — and admits to not catching on
very fast. That's why George yells at him. We'll see how long
he lasts.

* * * * *

AT NOON two "artist wives" arrived and ascended for
tea with the Australian gals. Mardi Ruoolo from Berkeley and
Janna Goodspeed from Croten Falls, NY.
Then in the evening, George made minestrone soup,
and the Ausies and I sat down to dine. George told us that
Hemingway wasn't really an expat — that none of the Lost
Generation could make that claim.
I changed the era, asked about Corso. George told us
that Corso had been banned from City Lights for burglarizing
Ferlinghetti. George said Corso had stolen from him as well:
an original *Ulysses*, and not just one, but two!
George was in a good mood and talking in a teeny-
weeny voice.

* * * * *

SOME GUY CAME IN last night and asked if George
still ran the joint. He told us that he had stayed here once a
decade ago and had been reading up in the Sylvia Beach when
he smelled a horrible burning smell — so went running out
to the corridor and found George standing there staring at his

reflection in the window with a candle in his hand and his hair in flames.

"Yeah," Constantin said, "he still cuts his hair that way."

* * * * *

OBSERVATION: Yesterday it hit me that Friar Morgan is a sad sad delusioned man and will soon suffer from a monumental deflation of expectations, something he will talk about for years as he continues to live amidst the lost souls and drifters here at Shakespeare.

For a few years now he's been writing a novel. The protagonist is an older man, a P.G. Wodehouse enthusiast enamored with a younger woman who fits the description of the mythical Pia — whom Morgan constantly and reverently refers to as "SHE" to anyone who will listen. So I do:

He is going to make her a very rich woman... and when they get to China, SHE will be a figurehead and worshipped like the Buddha... and Boy Oh Boy, you should see her dressed in leather pants!

Without a doubt, Friar Morgan is counting on Beijing, where he plans to establish a Shakespeare and Co. Reportedly, he has written a grant request to the Rockefeller Foundation in which he lists "Professor Goo, best friend of Professor Gaa" as his business associate there.

But the facts, I'm afraid, appear quite different. From what I hear from those who know Pia, she is twenty-one years old and merely amused by our friar's attention.

And if they're going to China to live together, where is she? And is this mademoiselle with 60-something years left in life willing to devote herself to the dream-schemes of a sad old man's fantasy world?

Hopefully, Morgan won't get burned too bad. For example, here's the way his friarmind operates: When his new vest got ripped off up in the Tumbleweed Hotel (aka, the Sylvia Beach), he lamented the difficulty in acquiring a new one. First, he would have to fly from Beijing to Hong Kong for $350 US, and then he'd have to spend $100 for the new vest, plus pay for accommodations and food and wine while waiting for the new one to be properly tailored with custom stitching. Then there's the time spent waiting, and another two or three thousand francs to get back to Beijing — all for a piece of fabric with some pockets on it.

So that's the scoop on Friar Morgan and it bothers me to write it because there's not an ounce of ill-will in the man, who has always been friendly and helpful to me. Nevertheless, this is a history and Morgan is a part of it. Unfortunately, like most people here who dream of transcending the way things are, the poor old guy has lost his mind.

* * * * *

THURSDAY SEPT 29, 1994: When "I" took on this project "I" was pretty psyched, because third-fiction NONFICTION, so I figured, would be a welcome change. I'd been working on two novels back in the States, both concerning MYSELF — such that it got to the point that I wanted to step outside MYSELF and write about fish or something. In fact, I was so sick of the subject of MYSELF that I actually did away with MYSELF. But as you can see, I'm at it again. In this text, "I" is everywhere.

So, until George does away with ME, or kicks ME out

or changes ME, this history will continue to be dominated by MY side of the story.

Thus, the future of this history is up to George, who told me many pages back to tell about MYSELF. So that's what I'm doing, figuring: If this turns into another self-reflective ME-tale, then I'll just file it away in the archives of MYSELF where it can fester among the other works waiting for the Quintessential Solar Flash to break on through the ruptured ozone and erase all data on the planet.

* * * * *

GEORGE HAD LUNCH YESTERDAY, charmed girlies gathered all around him. Harem-like, they were hugging him and serving him as he wound out stories with grand sweeping gestures. Even Kitty, the yellow cat, was focusing on George. Adoration filled the room.

"They chopped down the tree twice before," George told us (though me, specifically). "Once someone locked his bicycle to it and then the thief... the thief cut down the tree and got the bicycle... Get that down! And another time we poisoned it, poisoned the tree!"

Then George points to me.

"Him! He's our Historian, you know... he's writing this down, writing it all down! Huh, what's wrong? Don't you enjoy your job? All you have to do is write down everything... Absolutely Everything! It's a very very important job, because this is a very very historic place! You see, the French Government has pronounced us a *Monument Historique!*"

One of George's soft admirers suddenly asks if he bribed an official. A transition occurs which I miss.

"Blacksheep!" George cries out. "I'm the blacksheep

of the family! Oh Blacksheep, Blacksheep, Terrible
Blacksheep!"

And rising, he rushes to the nearest girly, kisses her,
and declares to us all, pointing at me:

"But he — he's going to make me a monster! Oh
Tragic Tragic Blacksheep Me!"

The gals giggle nubiley. We all know I'd sooner
make him the character he is, rather than the monster he's
not. It's ridiculous and George knows it, because we, as well
as thousands more, are his transitory family, and we love him
way too much to cast him out among the thistles. Besides,
this Eden is his.

"Oh poor poor blacksheep me," George laments, and
all the women rush to him. And as he vanishes beneath a
flurry of hugs and kisses, I hear him laughing "he he he..."

It's almost as if he's winking at me.

* * * * *

THAT AFTERNOON: I meet Moe in front of the
shop. Moe is a writer I met last year. We have mutual friends,
but we've never really hung out together. So we go to his
place and slug down a twelve-pack of 6.5% beer and cook a
chicken.

"Poetry is dead!" I argue, and give him the exact date
of its suicide. Moe, however, argues that it exists in Palestine.
We are not listening to each other. We're just shooting off our
mouths because we're bombed. Then we eat the chicken, get
on the Metro, and go to a squat on the edge of Père Lachaise.

John Blesso is doing a stand-up gig tonight. He's an
American comic who hangs at Shakespeare. I sit between
Moe and Tracy. They hate each other and amuse themselves

by talking openly about what a piece-of-shit the other one is.
Many daggers pass between them. We drink more beers.
Moe gets sloppy drunk.

After the show, Moe's hands are all over me.

"You've got a beautiful body," he tell me. "You're a
strong man."

"I'm just a whiteboy," I respond.

"I want to suck your dick. There comes a time when a
man has to make love with a man. A nice big pussy would be
good too, but I'd rather suck your dick. I bet you got a good
strong dick. It's okay for me to feel this way. I'm a homo. I
like bodies. I'm okay with that!"

"Well, that's really liberating for you," I tell him, and
smack his hands away, "but don't go getting gay with me."

Moe belches, blinks, wavers in the chair, and for the
next half hour, explains how much ecstasy he's gonna give me
when he sucks me off. Repeatedly, I tell him I'm not into that.
I tell him it's not an issue with me, so he should respect that.
But Moe won't change the subject.

And I don't wanna be mean, but I'm getting pretty
sick of this harassment. This always seems to happen to me:
aggressive gay guys bullying me because they gotta bust a
nut. In his face I see a sea of guys I should of told to go fuck
themselves. Just because I translate Genet doesn't mean I
wanna take it up the ass. I tell him:

"You make me wanna smash your face in when you
talk like that, Moe. And I don't wanna feel that way, cuz I don't
hate you yet."

"Oh, so you want to fight?" he asks, holding up two
fists like delicate buttercups. "You don't like me, huh?"

I look at his face. All it is is a sack of sorry alco-skin
with a layer of fragile bone beneath. With one punch I could

39

make him swallow half his teeth. His nose would be busted.
Then I'd hit his eggshell head. My fist would enter the center
of his brain. He'd swallow a sea of snot and blood.

I could murder him.

I want to murder him.

So I get up, grab my bag, and head to the Metro.

When I get back to Shakespeare, Constantin and
Steph and Majella and Hedvig from Sweden are juggling
outside. Now I'm home, where everything is sane.

Another night in Paris.

* * * * *

JACKAL, the white cat, is gone. Hasn't been seen for
days. No ransom note has been received yet.

* * * * *

PEOPLE TAKE ADVANTAGE of George's generosity.
Not only do his guests have a history of ripping him off, but
there are also those who don't pull their weight. For instance,
the two women from Malaysia and Singapore have been here
for a week and they still haven't done a lick of work. George
doesn't mind, though. The British have their princesses too.

Take this morning, for example: It was the second
day in a row in which I found myself opening the bookstore on
my own. Now, the thing is, when you open the store, there are
boxes of books that need to be hauled out, and I don't know
where they go. It would be ideal to share this chore with two
or three or four, of course, so then we'd all get yelled at.

This morning, Friar Morgan was puttering around
while I hustled butt, putting stuff in the wrong spots. Two or

three times I hinted to him that I'm gonna be the guy who's gonna get it, and two or three times he agreed with me. Then he said he was gonna go get a paper — when half the out-books were still in-books. So I exploded at the poor old guy:

"What are you talking about!? Okay! From now on, we gotta get those boys up and gettum moving, See! Everyone works! All Right!?"

Morgan nodded meekly, asking, "Can I go now?"

"YES!" I howled at a man at least twice my age. "GO!" And he went shuffling off.

So now I'm Cranky Guy.

Cranky Guy goes storming up to the Tumbleweed Hotel. Julian is in bed, lolling in his fartbag.

"You think I like being responsible in the morning!?" I yell at him, glimpsing George from the corner of my eye. "NO WAY IN HELL!" Then running down, I haul all the boxes out.

George comes out. Reorganizes. But he doesn't yell at me. Maybe he's getting a kick out of somebody else being the curmudgeon. I don't know. I go back upstairs and grab the typer while Friar Morgan and Julian and Ariel moon around scratching their arses.

"If I gotta be Responsible Guy," I tell them, "you can expect to hear me voice my distress!" They look at their shoes. Boy, their shoes sure are interesting. "IT WON'T HAPPEN AGAIN!" I command, slamming the door and stomping down to the park, where I type till way past noon.

Moral: The difference between pissing off a historian and pissing off someone who's not, is that when you piss off the person who isn't, his version of the story becomes distorted by memory alone and eventually fades. The historian's story, however, is subject to emotional bias and the tools he has at hand, so it stays a little longer. That's what happens. And it ain't a debatable issue either.

* * * * *

FRIDAY SEPT 30 1994: Two Israeli journalists were entertained by Steph yesterday up in George's palatial apartment — where in the afternoon I went to watch the BBC video of Shakespeare and Co entitled *Reams of Passion* — starring George Whitman, Allen Ginsberg, William Burroughs, and others. I watched it with the Australian gals, who kept sighing and saying how cute George is.

* * * * *

DISCOVERED THREE NOTES: The first two were written a week ago by the New Zealand women staying in the Antiquarian Shop. Before I went to the wedding, I showed them my "History File," and that's where they stashed them.

> *Dear Mark,*
> *Well first of all we would both like to thank you for letting us shack up in your room... our stay was brilliant... a real lively little hive, attracting many eccentric but thoroughly amusing characters... it was a pleasure to spend time here and I feel more inspired than ever...*
> *—Lisa Stevenson*

> *Dear Mark,*
> *I met a few people last night... One guy from America... had this watch that was quite*

remarkable. It was a Rolex face stuck onto
a solid silver bracelet in which were set very
ancient turquoise stones... I thought it was ugly
but I liked him and told him it was glorious.
Then I met another guy... he told me about his
friend who slept with Marilyn Monroe.
    —Merrin McLeod

The third note, however, was a frenzied note, jotted who-knows-when by George himself to his brother Carl. I found it on the floor beside the wastebasket:

Dear brother Carl,
This is the année terrible that can decide
the fate of S & Co. It is in serious danger of
disappearing. Could you drop everything
and come to the rescue? Would one or two
thousand dollars a month for two or three hours
of work per day cover your expenses? Before it
is too late, let's set up a foundation & thereby
carry on the good works...
    —Your blacksheep brother George

* * * * *

SATURDAY OCT 1, 1994: Jeffery, expatriate journalist/photographer, has fixed the typer, wherin this report from Julian Lord was discovered:

The position of Shakespeare and Company
Historian is a pernicious one indeed, living
among the people he writes about, he must

43

*inevitably conceive an intense dislike of most of
the regulars of the shop (given the extravagance
of our lunacies); an honest transcription of
events seen through his eyes can only be a
mixture of bilious presumptions, hatreds and
hypocrisy. A foul cocktail!*

*In the periphery of Shakespeare and
Company one notes the relentless passage of
the cyclical events which make up the heart of
the bookshop's life. The diffused light slowly
spreading into the library accompanies the
hushed roar of the Parisian traffic and tells us
all that morning has arrived.*

*George has purposefully not been
waking the guests to help the current historian
open up. Mark has therefore been clumsily
manoeuvering boxes and boards as George
screams at him, hounding him to do a proper
job, gleefully and sadistically treating him with
great injustice.*

*Yesterday, Mark blew his top and flew
through the library where we were still getting
dressed, before whining irrationally, and yes,
childishly, about how unfair it is that George
has __him__ do all the work and how __he's__ the only
one being flogged! Poor Mark...*

*We oldtimers do have some
indulgences for him, though; we have all been
victims of George's sado-homosexual urges and
have noted the gleam of pleasure in his eyes
as he forces one of his young male guests (and
it seems not much better with the fresh-faced,*

*inexperienced and effeminate ones) to whirl
about and do the work of two or three...*

*But Mark takes his revenge, of course,
in his history of the bookstore, and his judgment
is swift! So swift, indeed, that objective thought
and reasoned criticism make no appearance
in his vitriol. He savagely attacks Morgan's
tragic infatuation, not wondering if it may not
conceal something other than what is apparent;
never noticing Morgan's own laborious
savagery and cunning, then hypocritically ends
with some bleeding-heart nonsense about what
an intrinsically "good" person Morgan is.*

*But how ugly it is to attack people in
this fashion. I could, of course, make other
judgments of the same kind, but as Mark is the
historian, I will leave it to **him** to do all of the
flaying! Were his knife only a little sharper...*

*I shan't employ hypocrisy myself,
though; I harbor a long-standing illogical
loathing of Mark, one which is evidently
reciprocated; and am only contributing to
the store's history (at the behest of George) in
order to make my riposte against his own foul
writings.*

*In the meantime, George settles into
his captain's chair to stare through the picture
window at the beautiful young people milling in
the haze (dreaming perhaps of trees cut down?)
as customers come in, ask questions, buy books,
or steal.*

Then Karl comes in, and after a

*bit, Constantin, as everyone does the same
boring thing day after day... being polite to
George, to each other and the customers.
Perhaps not so polite to George's guests and
the Shakespeare hangers-on (personal likes or
dislikes aside, complete with sexual attractions
and aversions), while character faults drive the
instincts of commerce and George walks about
rubbing his hands, surveying the bubbling
transfigurations in his bookshop-shaped
alchemical laboratory; cackling as he sees a
temper flare, a rebel cowed — and discreetely
stealing away when he discovers someone
writing...*

*The guests return from their
occupations of the evening as the last customers
are herded out and Constantin prepares the
accounts. Boxes full of bargain books are
heaped on floors, bottles of wine swish around
in stomachs that could be better filled, shutters
are closed and the residents settle down in
bedbug blankets and sleep their way to another
day at Shakes and Co.*

* * * * *

RON FINE just walked in. He's gonna stay for
a week. He'll be working and studying in Paris for eight
months. He's an electronic composer from San Frisco.

Jeffery, on the other hand, was running around trying
to find George's missing letter to his brother. Luckily, I still
had it.

46

"Tell George you found it by the cashbox," I told him, and Jeffery got yelled at.

* * * * *

SUNDAY OCT 2, 1994: Jason came from the English Caribbean to get a job in the hotel biz, and Melinda Manos came from Wiltshire Village in search of "a new freedom, a valued existence and a new reality." Julian got drunk on redwine and puked in the sink, and the toilet pipes started leaking in George's upper chamber. Meanwhile, Majella fluted Pan-like as Constantin and I groveled amidst the drippage, all of us fretting the morrow and the wrath of George. Luckily, though, some mysterious act of somebody's god stopped the leak.

* * * * *

THE FLAPJACKS WERE A FLOP without George's scintillating presence. He just didn't feel like presiding with his spatula this week. George, also, wasn't seen at the tea party — which many young internationals did attend, ascending to the strange strange room that a strange strange man had invited them to.

George was a stranger today.

Hopefully, he's not sick — and sick of us. Sometimes it's impossible to tell. George's friend Claire from Waybackwhen, however, is here, and it is now reported that George is more *up* than earlier before.

* * * * *

Then Suddenly There's Violence Like Always
René Standing in the Doorway

I can feel the malnutrition
lack of vitamin C, broccoli

*

Majella flutes above the traffic
makes the night more beautiful
than silent

*

it makes me sick that we gotta get sick
I want to kiss her on the lips

... that's all

* * * * *

MONDAY OCT 3, 1994: Matt from Cally graduated college, took his Spam-fed white-bread ass to Paris and ended up in Ron Fine's bed because Julian was superchunking in the nightsink. Meanwhile, Will from Europe paints out front and another conflict arises:

Historian vs. History

Scenario:

Me (agitated): "I wonder about this history deal, George. Like, what's up?"

George: "Well, there's too much trivia in what you're writing! You want to sell it to another publisher? Go ahead! But you won't sell many copies and you won't sell any in this bookstore!"

Me: "Well, tell me what you want. I'll change it."

George: "You've written some more since the last batch, haven't you? So, let's see everything. Everything!"

I hand it over.

Me: "Maybe you're right, George. Maybe this isn't my job. What I'm concerned about are the Genet translations."

George (nodding nodding shooing me away): "Yes yes yes yes..."

then:

me sitting on the green slat bench
thinking about all
the details left out

— like how I sleep on a door-sized board raised off the floor to avoid the bedbug hordes as roaches swarm beneath...

— and Friar Morgan telling people he's 48, when everyone knows he's 60-something and leaving magazines out with pictures of stately senators and their young busty trophy wives...

— and the many myths about how George hides money in books, then tells me that it's true, and it is. Because I search for weeks until finally I find one stuffed with 2400 francs, so hand it back, asking:

"So, you're kinda like a squirrel, huh?"

And he shoots back:

"NO! MORE LIKE A MANIAC!"

Anyway, "pernicious," "trivial," "vitriol," whatever. It's now clear to George as well as me that I'm not gonna write what he wants me to — something I put to him today and he replied "I'll shake on that!" Then he advised "Stick to poetry, Old Boy."

And so

    this "history"

        is over.

P.S. George, the buckwheat quiche was good and all the gals were sad you weren't there, so they bestowed all their affection on me.

FAKOS IN FRANCE

Though I lived in Boulder for many years, I never met Ginsberg until I went to France. I was staying at the expatriate bookstore Shakespeare and Company where I was Writer in Residence (meaning I had a free place to stay and translate Genet) in the midst of drug addicts, drifters, and thieves — not to mention crazy old men like Friar Morgan (hopelessly in love with Princess Pia) and George Whitman, the whacky old guy who ran the joint.

And the Paris fall was toxic as always and damp and gray with pollution. There was a lot of exhaust and carbon monoxide. Walking outside was like peeling an onion. And it just kept dragging on. Winter was coming.

But suddenly there was excitement. Because one day George came bounding down the stairs in his faded maroon corduroy suit and punched me in the chest and cackled:

"Ginsberg's Coming! He'll be doing a reading! Yes, Yes! A reading from his new book by Penguin!"

Then he danced a jig out into the street, greeting Swedish ladies, talking charming to the Chinese, and asking Germans up for tea. It'd been five years since Ginsberg read at Shakespeare, so this was an excuse to break out the rum punch and have a party and everything!

Instantly, there were flags and banners all over the

place — along with Ginsberg's guru-face. His books were coming in from City Lights and everything was getting hyper.

Meanwhile, my publisher and I were scrambling to get my manuscript ready. I'd been working on it for almost three years. It was a new translation of Genet's verse and we were shooting to get the mighty blurb from Ginsberg.

Because one night when George was drunk at the till, I walked in and he jumped up and said:

"Salutations, Old Boy! What can I do for you? Just name it, Old Boy! I'm putty in your hands!"

"Well," I asked him, "can you get your buddy Ginsberg to blurb me?"

And "Sure thing, Old Boy!" George said. "Ginsberg? Genet? Why Ginsberg loves Genet! Slept with him even! Yes, Yes! You can count on me, Old Boy!"

Still, I didn't care to see Ginsberg read — since I'd already seen him at the Boulder Theater sitting down there in a straight-back chair, head wobbling around like a bobber on a spring, reading "Kaddish." It cost me ten bucks — and I wasn't impressed. I mean, there he was in front of thousands and thousands of Naropa/University people OOOOOOOOOOOing and AWWWWWWWWWWWWing as if he were God when it was totally clear they were buying his theatrics hook, line and sinker. What was really stunning, though, was his howling self-confidence as he spouted off words with such masterful precision that envy was actually rising like a hardcock. Butchya know what? Any cocky screamer could've screamed what Ginsberg screamed that night, and that's what I kept thinking.

These are the words which came to my mind: *Word-Charlatan! Performer! Trickster! Harlequin!*

And maybe it was jealousy, but maybe it was

something else. Like maybe I could see right through him. But how could this be? I mean, he's "The Master" — the guy who wrote "Howl" — the only Visionary Poet of the Century (so some claim) — who used to run with Kerouac and Corso and Burroughs and Dylan — all those guys. And he made a legend of himself and he didn't even have to die to do it. Because he's the guy who ran ranting in the streets (at night amidst monoliths) that he had heard the Great Prophetic Voice of Blake! So who was I to think him a shyster? I mean, if I put Ginsberg down that must mean I think I'm better than him — right?

Anyway, these were the thoughts that kept going through my head — which I didn't want in my head — yet I wanted to meet him. Dreaded it even — felt that I should. Plus, I wanted the blurb.

In the meantime, Larz Larsen and I were illegal aliens painting apartments for Lady. We'd show up at nine and by noon we were drunk. Lady would bring us wine and drink it with us giggling. She'd pay us 50 francs an hour and we'd paint away. We'd do all her walls, and sometimes her husband Zen Lunatic would come on in with a big wheel of cheese. So we'd paint and paint and listen to my only tape: REO Speedwagon singing "Riding the Storm Out" (the live long version) over and over and over again.

Larz was a goat-bearded filmmaker from Northern Cally and was excited to meet Ginsberg (whom he kept calling "The Angelheaded Hipster"), but I was bummed that we couldn't go running through the Negro streets at dawn, laughing hysterical naked like Ginsberg did — because we had to work! Like most artists everywhere! My point being: Whereas "Howl" was the epic poem of the Beat Generation, "Haul" should be the poem of ours. So Larz was joking I should write it — but I'd just shout it out instead, painting at Lady's:

"I SAW THE BEST IMAGINATIONS OF MY GENERATION DESTROYED BY STAGNANCE — THOUGH WELL-FED AND MAKING IT, LIVING IN LANDFILLS IN CONDOS IN TOWNHOMES — DRIVING AM/FM/CD MACHINES TO UNIVERSITIES FOR DEGREES AND CUBEROOMS IN THE CITY WHILE SCRAMMING TO BEND OVER FOR SOME DUMB GRUNT JOB — SLOBBING SWEATING GREASING SCRUBBING TORQUING WRENCHING ALWAYS HAULING! HAULING BOXES, HAULING PIANOS, HAULING COUCHES, HAULING STEREOS! AND CORNDOGS AND PEPSI AND COKE AND COCAINE! KURT COBAIN!! HAULING HAULING HAULING HAULING! THE MOBIUS STAIRWAYS! BY THE HOUR! FOR THE DOLLAR! HAULING GRASS, HAULING ASS, HAULING WITH A COLLAR — "

And on and on and on like that. Each time it came out different.

But then one day in the midst of the hype, I met him face to face. I was walking and talking, eating falafel (as was my habit: migrate/masticate/memorize) and heading down these pee-smelling stairs at St. Michel, over toward the Beat Hotel (or what used to be the Beat Hotel) and there he was: The Great Ginsberg!

But he didn't look like I thought he would — ie, shaggy beard and plump and stuff (to tell the truth, "a trim little fag" is what I thought), but it was him alright. Yep, definitely him. Because as I took him in — that thin Jewish nose, those thick liver-lips, everything Ginsberg about him — I saw him stop and watch my reaction, seeing everything

54

I saw the instant I saw it. So he paused, waiting for me to say whatever it was I had to say.

But I wouldn't. Nope. I wasn't gonna kiss his gilded ass! So I glanced at his golden boy beside him, who was also waiting for me to say what I had to say (I must have had my mouth wide open) — but still I wouldn't. I just shifted my glance back to Ginsberg and stood there staring. But what's he gonna do — just stand there all day? Hell no! He kept on walking.

So I had to say something. Because I couldn't just meet him like this and not say nothing. I'd kick myself for the rest of my life. So I yelled the first thing that came to mind:

"PERT BUTTOCKS UPRAISED FOR MY MASTERFUL RAPE WHICH WERE MEANT FOR A PRIVATE SHIT IF THE ARMY WERE ALL!!"

(a line of his which had lodged itself inside my mind like a piece of corn between the teeth the day I first discovered it)

But Ginsberg just kept walking.

So I went to Hell — or Enfer, rather — which is the oldest porno collection in France, down in the bowels of the Bibliothèque Nationale — and studied "The Galley" (Genet's third known poem) for the ten millionth time, before eventually heading back to Shakespeare.

Where my publisher was working the register, so I asked him:

"Did Le Fat Daddy come on in?"

And "Yes," he said, "as a matter of fact, he just stopped by with his little Adonis. Then stood there, as always, looking around, before asking where his books were."

"Then what?"

"I told him 'We don't stock your little books anymore.

There's no demand for them anymore.'"

I laughed and went upstairs. To see George — who's 80-something years old, but jumping all around:

"You just missed him, Old Boy! He just came by! Came by for lunch!"

I looked on the table. My manuscript was there right next to the beer.

"Didjya get it?" I asked.

"Didn't get drunk enough, Old Boy!" George said, and socked me in the chest again.

* * * * *

Then more hype, more energy rising, as the famous day approaches. George is putting up posters from ten years back: Michael McClure doing poetry in Frisco. Gary Snyder giving a lecture. Diane di Prima! Ferlinghetti! It was looking like a Beat convention.

And suddenly George isn't sick anymore. Before that, he'd been coughing and hacking. But now he's glowing — and taking those big ridiculous emu-steps and constantly dining with "girlies." And his chin's up high and he's wearing his brand- new bright red pajamas (and not just in the bookstore, but at the bank and the market and all over Paris). And every morning there's a knock on my door. And every morning there's a girly standing there with a big tray of breakfast. Because George is sending down fruit and oatmeal and big loaves of bread so huge I take em and eat em all day. He's treating me like a king — like he never treated me before.

"It's because you're his poet," my publisher says, "and he's intending on presenting you to Ginsberg."

But George doesn't have to. Because one day I'm down there in the Rare Book Room (which is my room) and I look out the window. And there he is. And Golden Boy too. Both of em standing there and leaning way back and looking way up, regarding the building as if it's the past — but now he's back.

So I rush out to talk to him. I tell him "PERT BUTTOCKS UPRAISED FOR MY MASTERFUL RAPE WHICH WERE MEANT FOR A PRIVATE SHIT IF THE ARMY WERE ALL!" again, and await his response.

"Now wait a second," Ginsberg tells me. "Repeat what you just said."

So I say it again — but before I'm even half-way through he raises his hand:

"Slower," he tells me (as if I'm so starstruck I'm outta control), "slower... slower..."

I say it again. Slower.

"Hmmmmmmm," Ginsberg hmmms. "Not 'Pert.' I wouldn't have used 'pert.' Pert? No. Not pert."

"Yes," I tell him, "yes pert."

"Hmmm, no... not pert. No, definitely not pert. Perhaps stern, but not pert. I wouldn't have used pert. No. Not pert."

"Yes pert."

"Not pert."

The argument goes nowhere. Golden Boy backs away. Ginsberg looks at me — asks:

"I hear it's George's birthday today. How old is he anyway?"

And I don't know how he knows I know George when I'm just some guy who approached him on the street. But I say "82 or 84... he won't tell us exactly."

57

"Well, he called me this morning and told me to come by and wish him a happy birthday."

"It is..." I tell him, "George's birthday."

We fall into silence. I don't give a rat's ass for him and he doesn't give a shit about me — so wanders over to the 10-franc books while I go back to translating.

But I can't — not with Ginsberg out there.

Again, I look out the window. He's heading into the store. So I rush out and follow him in and everyone gathers around. It's a big big scene with people crowding in. And George in the center is eating his dinner (big globs of butter) and ordering girlies "Go Get This person! Go Get That Person!" and everyone's waiting for Ginsberg to say what he's gonna say. And then he (the man whose greatest accomplishment, according to himself, was bringing Zen Buddhism to America) says:

"Your diet is shit, old man."

All hell breaks loose. Pia pisses a puddle of perfumed pee. Roy and Morgan sway in time. George jumps ten feet in the air. Ted Joans guffaws. Flashbulbs flash —

* * * * *

FLASH: Here's the dope on Ted Joans, whose poser history goes back to his bongo-playing days when he used to rent himself out as "a negro for parties," according to numerous biographies he managed to weasel into — always saying he's a friend of Baraka or the #6 Beat. Once he even told a *Boston Globe* reporter how he and Kerouac used to be best pals, and she actually sent this to press. Because Ted Joans is the kinda guy who's always sticking his head into pictures — but I know him mostly through Shakespeare, where he's always showing up in fashion hats and fashion pants — with Clonia, his female companion (always wearing the exact same outfit) — and then they go around smiling those big cheese-grins and shaking hands and laughing loudly — presiding over every social situation up in the Sylvia Beach — always smiling smiling smiling "Hi, I'm Ted Joans. Hi, we're Ted Joans." Because they're part of the Jim Haynes butt-sucking club — who erect monuments to themselves by publishing chapbooks about themselves, for themselves, by themselves — which is Handshake Press — which is responsible for the flimsy copy of *Duck Butter Poems* up in George's topmost apartment — wherein Ted Joans inscribed his gratitude to George for all the WOMEN he's met at Shakespeare: Black WOMEN, white WOMEN, nymphos, nuns, "even a witch!" All sorts of WOMEN — before going on to note how he's done more readings at Shakespeare than anyone else and how he brought Black History to France and Blah Blah Blah Blah Blah.

Lately, though, most people know Ted Joans for the same tired poem he keeps repeating whenever he gets the chance to perform it (which I'll repeat shortly, since it makes its way into this story) —

* * * * *

But back to the Mayhem, the Chaos, the bookstore flashing on and off. It's like there's a kettle drum banging away — as if giant gongs are reverberating:

"THE KING HAS RETURNED!!
WELCOME BACK, KING!!
THE KING IS BACK!!

I can hardly stand it — the phoniness, the glory for
the sake of glory — the same sorta glory with which Khomeni
was welcomed back to Iran! Senseless Nationalism! Religious
Convictions! The treating of an individual as if he were God —
when, in fact, we all take dumps and we all have evil/selfish/
not-nice thoughts, because no one's a saint and no one's a
rockstar — not even rockstars! I mean, it's the propaganda,
not the artist, which people react to. It's so fucking stupid, it's
so fucking lame! Because if everyone is supposedly equal,
why is he a deity and therefore above the flock that put him
where he is for pointing out how HOLY HOLY HOLY we are?

And then I see Beauty rolling her eyeballs and
pushing through the crowd. Beauty is my gal. We go
scramming off to Lady's.

* * * * *

Lady lets me use this flat whenever I want to spend
the night with Beauty. The ceilings are high and the rafters
are ancient and there's a bed and it's clean and no roaches and
no bedbugs, the whole place smelling like fresh paint.

We take off our clothes and get in the tub. Beauty
has small breasts. I love her. I don't know why I love her
— maybe it's because she loves me.

Anyway, we drink wine and talk about "fakos" putting
on shows at Shakespeare — and over at Handshake — and
Everywhere! And eating it up!

And Beauty's surprised to hear me say I don't want to
be that way — and glad to hear it also. Her cheekbones ride
high as she smiles in the tub, telling me:

"I've been worried you wanted to live like that."

"No way," I say. "By tricking others into thinking I'm hotshit? So as to rub elbows with fakos! Fakos among fakos! Fakos trying to impress each other with *Divine Inspired Genius*! Hell no! I don't wanna hang out with Fakos. Getting backslaps from dickwads and dorkheads who go parading their selfish selves around, seeking affirmation from strangers so as not to die in fear of what they fear most: that they will go and croak unknown! Cuz all that — that's bullshit! That's not real. Ginsberg's holy ass — that's not real! Yucking with Ted Joans — that's not real! Whatta buncha crap that is! I mean, you — you're real. And I would rather run with you, beautiful you, beautiful beautiful not fake you."

> *Beauty naked in the tub*
> *Beauty naked wet with suds*
> *she's so real, she's my gal*
> *actually wants me*
> *to call her "my gal"*

"I'm your gal," she tells me. "Call me your gal."

"You're my gal," I say.

She's the sweetest gal on the planet — has a nose like a rabbit's. It scrunches up funny when she smiles in the tub — and it looks like a grimace, but it's not.

Somehow, the subject changes. I don't know how, or why, but I remember exactly what she says. She says:

"If you can love somebody in spite of your differences... then that's the most important thing."

> *And I am blowed away*
> *I didn't know*

61

she could be

so beautiful

It's the most intelligent thing I've heard all day, all week, all year, maybe in my life. And I want her forever — to hog for myself and nobody else — because she's *true* — in the truest sense of "being true" (even if this is a cliché).

The word "softwife" comes to mind.

I want Beauty for my softwife.

* * * * *

Then comes the day of the Fabulous Reading — when George comes running up, grabs my arm, and leads me through the various bookrooms, saying:

"I'm sorry, Old Boy, I apologize, apologize! Very very sorry, Old Boy! I asked him, but he said No. No No No! Absolutely No! He won't do any work in Paris! No No No No No! I don't know why he's like that! He used to be a real nice guy — used to help young writers all the time! Used to help them all the time!"

"That's okay," I reply.

George looks at me askewly. Then says:

"Come on, Old Boy! We've got work to do!"

George swings me through the Tumbleweed Hotel. We're linked by the elbows and he's shouting at drifters to "Clean this!" and "Scrub that!" And then he makes me grab the amp and we're down in the Antiquarian Shop — to practice his speech:

(Note: Most of the following comes from my tape recorder, which was running from this point on to the end of the reading)

62

"Something something something..." George says, "similar to the publication of *Leaves of Grass*... in 1956 when 'Howl' was first published... Allen Ginsberg... Allen Ginsberg... can you hear me, Old Boy?"

"Yeah yeah, George, I can hear ya."

He practices and practices as I adjust the knobs on the amp. It squelches, it squeaks — but I find the right place. The dials are touchy. It takes a long time. But I crank it up as loud as it goes — both of us goofing, having one hell of a time together. In fact, having the best time we've ever had together.

But I'm wondering why George is being so jolly, when usually we're so used to each other that we just do our own thing and never stop to play. Like cold afternoons in the Rare Book Room while George does the books and I translate away — neither of us saying nothing to the other. For hours and hours, notta ding-dang word passing between us. But then I find out why: We're on stage!

Turning around, I see 300 people staring through the huge picture window. Hundreds of people looking at us, standing on things, trying to get a glimpse of us.

And the next thing I know, Ginsberg arrives, so George is rushing me outside and I'm setting up the amp. And then the show is suddenly going and I'm standing next to Ginsberg and George — performing! Because now my role is... Little Amp Boy!

And Goddamnit, I feel like an idiot! I never intended on being here crammed in next to George and Ginsberg, hundreds of people ogling us. The three of us. And everyone knowing who they are, but no one knowing who I am — so figuring I must be some kinda buttboy.

George goes into his speech:

63

George: "Allen Ginsberg... Allen Ginsberg, he lived with... uhhhh... Allen Ginsberg and William Burroughs in the Beat Hotel... the Beat Hotel... just three doors down the street from Shakespeare and Company... Allen Ginsberg... he was a habitué of our library upstairs... and one day... one day Allen Ginsberg... decided he wanted to give a poetry reading... but he was a little bit shy... had to have a few drinks before he faced the audience..."

Ginsberg: "I never drink!"

The audience laughs.

And I'm proud of George. George is my hero and this is his moment. He's been waiting five years for this exact moment and now it's that moment. So he's belting it out with his teeny-weeny old man voice. And it's hard on him, it's draining him — I can tell. He has to yell real real loud even though the amp is cranked to the max.

Then Ginsberg! He reaches right over, starts messing with the knobs. He screws them all up, turns the volume all the way off. So suddenly George is howling out nothing. His great great speech, which I listened to him memorize — is nothing. Because no one can hear him. Except, that is, for Ginsberg and me and my tape recorder:

George: "And ummmmm... in those days our bookstore was just a hole in the wall, not a third of the size it is today... but now, of course... Allen Ginsberg is entitled... uhhh... accustomed to facing customers all the way from Peking to Prague..."

The crowd laughs. They're laughing at Ginsberg, still messing with the dials. And wiggling his ass. Fiddling away, fucking it up. There's feedback, distortion. And then he puts the knobs right back where I had em in the first place.

George: "...and we all welcome Allen Ginsberg back...

to read... in our bookstore in Paris... where he... [* garble ~ garble @ garble *] gave his first... very very first... poetry reading!"

Applause.

Ginsberg: "Okay. Now, can you hear in the back? Yeah. What's the best way? Direct? Straight on like this? Yeah. Okay."

Ginsberg pauses long and dramatic, then announces the name of his first poem as if heralding royalty into the room:

"Cosmopolitan...
.............................Greetings!"

Then George takes off, so I'm standing up there next to Ginsberg. I don't know why I'm standing next to Ginsberg — since I'm not even Little Amp Boy anymore.

Ginsberg: "Cosmo... uhhhh... do you know the association with the word 'Cosmopolitan'?... uhhh... it was Stalin's characterization of Jews... *úte les cosmopolitans* [or something like that] as you may remember. So these are cosmopolitan... Yiddish... greetings. You see, I was invited to Macedonia to receive a golden wreath at their evening of poetry, and they asked for some sort of..."

So why am I here, I'm asking myself, *standing next to Ginsberg like some sorta moron grinning this stupid appropriate grin?*

He goes into his poem:

"Stand up against governments,
 against God
 Stay irresponsible
 Say only what we know and imagine
 Absolutes are coercions
65

Change is absolute
Ordinary mind includes
eternal perceptions
How?

Observe what's vivid
Notice
What we notice..."

And on and on and on like that in slow simple syllables
— none of that howling fury from way back when in the
days of adolescent passion — Nope! Because now he's
chanting mantras, pulling New Age haikus, being abstract and
uncolorful!

And he's reading in that curvy way, that rising happy
jovial way, ending each line on an upward stress — like he
did on that *Dharma Bums* tape I listened to at the plastic
factory — which he slaughtered! Yes! Ginsberg slaughtered
Kerouac's prose with that same stupid senseless Zenjoy tone
he's affecting now — which'd make Kerouac barf up his guts.
I mean, Kerouac never wrote in a tone that wasn't his own —
and since he never found the glee which Ginsberg is affecting
now, he died a sad sick alcoholic.

Anyhow, Ginsberg goes on to equate himself with
Walt Whitman — but that's just standard truck for him. Like
condescending to the audience.

Ginsberg: "Uhhhh... Creely... anybody here know
Creely's work?"

And, of course, no one goes raising his hand like
some eager tot who knows the name of some dumb color.

Ginsberg: "Not so many people here know Creely,
huh? Come on. Okay... Robert Creely... major American

poet..."

I think about Ginsberg. I think about his poems.
How they ain't complex with rhythm no more — how they
no longer have that fire inside em — but rather, how they're
these quaint cute sing-song things. Little ditties with dates
and times written right after — as if recording the moment
divinity hit him and riding that "first word, best word" wave
— which is a lie!

Because when Ginsberg does that, what he's really
saying is "Kerouac Christ." Because, in essence, he's using
this myth to found a religion in which Kerouac is Jesus
— therefore fostering the illusion that *On the Road* was written
in two weeks. So let's get this straight: *On the Road* wasn't
just whipped up on a big roll of paper — there were plenty
revisions and it took ten years to write. And if you don't
believe me, just read Ginsberg's own words in a book called
Heart Beat by Carolyn Cassady, where he has this to say about
an early draft of *On the Road*:

"A lot of meaningless bullshit I think page after
page of surrealist free association that doesn't make sense to
anybody except someone what has blown Jack."

Anyway, I listen and listen and listen — all these
people looking at me. *Why the fuck are they looking at me?
I don't like em looking at me. I don't even like his poems
anymore. I think they suck. And he's a fako. Fuck this shit!*

I go to the periphery, drink redwine with Beauty,
smoke blackhash with friends. And then, when the reading
finally ends, Ted Joans jumps on in, gets right next to
Ginsberg, and drops his trademark poem:

"If you should see
A man

67

Walking down the street
Talking to himself
Do not turn
And run away
For this man
Is a poet
And you have nothing to fear
From a poet
But..."

There's a big long dramatic pause before he delivers
the punchline:

"The Truth!"

Lots of applause. The naïve and impressionable join
in clapping for brilliance.

"BULLSHIT!" I hear somebody shout. "TOTAL
BULLSHIT!" — then realize it's me.

Gotta get outta here, I figure.

But first I need to lock the bookroom up. So I haul
the cords and amp inside, grab my dirt-green duffel bag
(overpacked with all my stuff — my sleeping bag and dirty
socks, dictionaries and idiom books), but when I turn to leave,
someone slaps a bench down, barring my way. Then Ginsberg
sits down and Ted Joans slides in as the mob surges forth and
a table appears and a pile of books is stacked on top. It all
happens in less than two seconds.

So now I'm standing there and trapped there with a
hundred pounds crushing me down and Ginsberg and Ted
Joans and 400 people waving their books like swords in the
air. So I take my big black boot and I stick it in there — I jam
it in there — right between Ginsberg and Ted Joans. Who
squeal as I hoist my bag above my head like a big side of beef

and yell "BOMB THREAT!" and go lurching out, crushing feet, knocking piles of books to the ground as the crowd parts, laughing in my wake:

"Bomb threat!" they chant. "Bomb threat! Haaawwww! Haaawwww!"

Then I find Beauty and she takes my hand and we go scramming off to Lady's to spend together my last night in France.

* * * * *

Beauty's bleeding so much we can't make love. She's apologetic and she hates her tampon, but we get naked anyway and Beauty sucks me off instead.

Then lapping away at her tender red flesh, I tug on the string and probe with my tongue, her menstrual salts like wine in my mouth as I bury my face in the soft of her sex and waves shudder through her.

And the next day, I'm kicking my way to Charles de Gaule after having left George some hogwash note about how "Words aren't meant for the stroking of egos. They're meant for revolution. But thanks for the space to translate Genet."

Like I said: "hogwash."

Then boarding a plane and reading Céline, I'm flying back to New York City because I can't afford to stay with Beauty. So I left — like everyone everywhere who goes and blows it, then blames it all on something else.

SPITZER ON SPITZER ON CÉLINE

Before I went to France to translate Genet, all I knew about
Leo Spitzer was that he was my grandfather's cousin and a
big deal scholar of Romance Languages at Johns Hopkins.
There was a family story about how he came to dinner once,
and my father and uncle (who were kids at the time) behaved
"abominably." Whatever they did, though, was never made
clear — but it probably had to do with not treating a world-
famous linguist/literary critic with the proper degree of
respect my grandparents considered appropriate.

(They were Viennese Jews who had escaped the
Holocaust. My grandfather was a syphilis doctor and my
grandmother was the first woman to earn a degree from the
University of Vienna. So they took things seriously)

Four decades later I met Albert Dichy, the French
expert on Genet, as well as the curator of the IMEC Archives
(the French center for research on "contemporary literature")
in Paris. When I walked in, I was wearing torn-up jeans and
a tie-dyed t-shirt — so I didn't appear very professional,
or anything like a scholar, as my gold-stamped letter of
introduction from the University of Minnesota attested I was.
But as soon as Monsieur Dichy read my name, and as soon
as I affirmed that I was indeed related to the highly lionized
Leo — POW! WANG! ZINNNNNGG! They served me lunch,

gave me champagne, and rolled out the red carpet! Leo's reputation had earned me the key! Instantly, I was awarded access to all their rare books as well as a personal introduction to Edmund White himself, who appeared in the instant — so we went out for coffee.

Edmund White had just written that monolithic book on Genet and it was coming out all over the planet. Paris was abuzz with hype: Genet at the newsstands, Genet at the theater, Genet on posters everywhere! A big Genet conference was coming up at the Pompidou Center, a new play was being released, and Edmund White was at the center of it all — and willing to help me on my project! We talked prison argot. Reform-school argot. Pedarest slang. And then he told me more about Leo — how he's known and revered in different countries for different studies, though in France he's considered a hero for his work on Céline.

Who I soon got into. I was impressed by *Death on the Installment Plan* and the crazy flipped-out tempo of the story. Céline was mad — authentically mad — and his madness had form. In essence, Céline had created his own private language, which didn't care about what was expected.

So I studied Céline, laughing my ass off. And then I found the songs, some poems, some obscure prose, and a never-before-translated play. I got to work. And years later, I went looking for an article by Leo on Céline. It was published in *Le Français moderne*, June 1935, and was entitled "Une Habitude de style (le rappel) chez Céline" (which I translated as "A Stylistic Practice of Céline"). And since it hadn't been translated yet, I went to town.

But let's face it: Linguistics is boring because linguists are boring. And loyalty is stupid, especially in families. So I don't care what Harold Bloom and others have

72

to say about what a magnificent thinker Leo was,[1] I'm going to tell it like I see it — since every generation is a bit more abominable than the one that came before it.

("Abominable," incidentally, comes from the Old English spelling of "abhomynable," in which the Latin root "ab homine," means *away from man*)

This is how I see it: My translation of "Une Habitude" is not important. It's not worth my energy to present it, and it's not worth anyone suffering the rhetoric to read it. However, there are two significant terms which Leo Spitzer examines (by building on theories of M. Vendryes, M. Sandfeld, and M. Bally), before using the fiction of Céline to illustrate how common speech becomes a stylistic technique:

Le Tour: (or the turn-of-phrase) is a phrase split into at least two parts, in which the subject is discovered at the end of the phrase where it seems to be out of place — as in this excerpt from *Journey to the End of the Night*: "I bet that made him feel good, the bastard!"[2]

Leo Spitzer explains that in this specific case there are two peaks of intensity: one resting on the objective statement, and the other on the critical remark. The epithet, of course, supplies a judgmental value — which makes for a rhythm of thought in the author's work that alternates between these peaks with a pure simple enunciation playing upon the reader's conviction.

Le Rappel: is then defined as the return of discourse to one of its parts, which introduces a reflective element into language, since the repetition of a subject works to install it as a concept for readers.

The rappel's effect on tone is then discussed by Leo Spitzer, who draws upon the example of Céline repeating "The Mayor" in a certain passage, rather than providing a pronoun to quell the attention Leo Spitzer claims the Mayor's title constantly provokes. Leo Spitzer then establishes how the repetition of this title colors all inclusive sentences with the subject's beingness, thus providing (according to Leo Spitzer) an omnipresence.

Dig?

After this, Leo Spitzer goes on to describe a whole slew of tours and rappels, as well as relative segmented phrases, random binaries and even a tour à rappel — all the while citing Céline. Leo Spitzer also refers to a certain "nuance" intrinsic in the stylistic practice of the rappel, which makes Céline's metaphoric voyage to the end of himself apparent through gestures and oaths in the text.

I'll sum up the rest: Flaubert is brought up, Rilke is addressed, and Schnitzler is quoted. Many more terms are expounded and defined.

This, however, is what I have to add to Leo Spitzer's observations (though not for the express purpose of "canon bashing" — which, no doubt, will be the popular assumption made about my motives here):

The Twist on the Turn: by creating an appositive in which the subject is colored with the author's experience or perspective (ie, "the bastard!"), the reader leaves the phrase influenced by the author's bias — which is a stronger way of ending a phrase than with an image or action that only retains minimal associations. Thus, Céline provokes a reaction; and because Céline is extreme, this reaction leads to empathy, or its exact opposite. A noun powered by argot, for instance, is emotional punctuation in itself, no matter where it occurs. Hence, the placement of that noun at the end of a phrase, rather than at the beginning, provides for extra punctuation. And for all the pontificating Leo Spitzer's done about semantic tactical style, it's curious that he didn't note this strategy of emphasis.

But this is typical of what the theorist misses when he attempts to deconstruct the artist. I mean, the point isn't that Céline was using some binary oscillating rhythm of everyday speech to map out style; the point is that the tour is a method of stress, and by stressing itself at the tail end of a phrase it succeeds in leaving the reader with a phantom which lingers in some form or another (and the strongest kind of phantoms, of course, are those with unperceivable presences). It's an old old trick, somewhat along the lines of ending a poetic line on an up-stress rather than a flat one. And it all boils down to a formula as simple as this:

For maximum effect, whether words be spoken or written, don't end a phrase on some lame note — end it with WANG DANG DOODLE!!!"

Céline realized this. My distinguished great-avuncular relation, however, did not.

Still, I don't completely understand — nor do I want to understand — the jargonistic labyrinth of the high-faluting mumbo-jumbo that ol' uncle Leo is respected for illustrating so lucidly. It's a right brain/left brain sorta thing, I figure, this dichotomy.

As for the rappel: The greatest irony in all of this has to do with an élitist self-righteousness which Leo Spitzer notes in others, but fails to see in himself. For example, in describing the tension between the quite personal and the socially comprehensible peaks of a segmented phrase, Leo Spitzer comments that when spoken language relies on correction (ie, "Hasn't the policeman caught him yet, his thief?"), it fabricates a pattern in the instant through a type of expression that doesn't feel certain — such that "This type of expression presents itself almost automatically with the 'bellyacher' attitude, which parodies the cruel words of propaganda." Adding: "These rappels are clearly common and infantile. The common man or child who doesn't know, and is afraid of not constructing phrases well, inserts rappels."

Still, I wouldn't criticize Leo Spitzer for noting our tendency to repeat ourselves to make a point, ya know? And I wouldn't criticize him for demonstrating this technique by repeating the various types of rappels there are. I just find it ironic.

Or, as Céline might've suggested through the *Rappeling Rappel* (my term) — which I envision was his vision and main stylistic technique (stacking itself upon itself, so therefore reaffirming itself by constantly referring to itself and creating manic motion):

"I just find it contradictory! Paradoxical! Nonsensical! Topsy-Turvy! Absurd!"

END NOTES

1. In Bloom's *The Western Canon* (Harcourt Brace & Company, 1994), he writes that Leo Spitzer is "one of the double handful of scholarly modern critics who matter," p. 491. This is typical of the automatic veneration Leo Spitzer often receives.

2. Ralph Manheim's translation, New Directions, NY, 1983, p. 34. It should also be noted that Leo Spitzer commented on how Céline often refused to separate the *segmented phrase* with commas, and that this technique indicates that his reversal of the subject and action is conscious.

All translations of Leo Spitzer in this essay by Mark Spitzer.

LOOKING FOR A WHORE TO FUCK

I was 29 years 364 days old, and there was a bald spot growing on the back of my head. I was on my way to the Czech Republic because I couldn't figure out what else to do. I only had a few hundred dollars to my name, I was in debt up to my asshole, and I couldn't find a job except for killing trees in Minnesota — which is what I'd been doing for the past few months.

Thirty years old is supposed to be a turning point — but so far nothing had changed. I was still running from city to city and country to country. It wasn't a romantic life; it was a pitiful life.

But I also had something else on my mind: I wanted to fuck a whore.

Yep! I hadn't had any for over six months and there was this fantasy that just kept going through my head, and the star of each show was an anonymous ass. A womanly callipygian ass. It was facing me and going up and down. And I was lying on my back and gripping that ass and staring into the arc of its back — which was bending back, because I was fucking what was under it. There was no face, no person, no love. Just that fine fine derriere and my hardcock in its slick heat.

At first, though, it kind of horrified me to realize I'd

be willing to pay for what I couldn't get on my own — because I'd always been a guy who got it for free. And it's not like I believed in throwing down dough for prostitution. In fact, I'd spent quite a lot of time debating that kind of exploitation, as well as wondering about guys who go porking chicks without affection. But then I got to thinking about how Kerouac used to sometimes fuck a whore, and I realized I wasn't in such bad company. Besides, it made me feel sleazy to do the taboo — and the thought of this turned me on — or, at least, I thought that it should, since it turned Bataille and Genet and Sade on. So I took it as a personal challenge to find a slut to fuck.

My plane landed in Amsterdam. And since I had a few hours to burn before leaving for Prague, and since I was once again in this "city of sin," and since I was feeling shameless and determined, I stashed my bags in a locker and took off for the Red Light District. This was my plan: First I was going to get fucked up, then I was going to fuck a whore.

So I went to a rasta coffee shop and ordered a beer and a spliff. The spliff was fat and full of hash. I drank the beer and smoked the spliff, and immediately felt tired. I didn't feel high, I didn't feel happy, I just felt tired. And then in the mirror across from me, I saw my reflection. And it was the reflection of an old haggard loser.

Bob Marley, however, was behind that loser, smoking a hooter. It was a mural on the wall. But for some reason, Bob didn't feel as crummy as me. There were rays of light shooting from his head. What he was projecting was Total Stoned Glory, a feeling I couldn't sympathize with. Because having smoked pot for over half my life, I was a burn-out.

But I had an idea: I'd start anew as soon as I turned thirty. According to my plan, this was the last day of my pathetic drug-life. Soon I'd be that guy I always wanted to be, who wasn't always looking for pot and didn't miss it when it was gone. After I fucked a whore, that is.

Then I went out and wandered around looking for a strumpet to fuck me. A lot of them were old and fat with saggy tits and rotten teeth. I, of course, desired a foxy young whore. A whore of beauty and contours — with a nice ripe ass and a succulent sex. I desired the finest whore in town. And then I saw her.

She was standing behind a window right on the main canal in front of the floating copshop. She was blonde with bursting nubile curves and she was just sort of dancing there in black lace with her boobs pushed up, enticing with a siren smile.

Man! This whore was all buttocks and breastwork and boobification. She was bountiful and buxom and busting with bubblicity. She was bouncing around with a bodacious bosom. Ba-ba-ba-booom! What a bimbo! She was the hottest whore I'd ever seen and I intended to bone her.

But shit! I suddenly felt like some dumb teenager working up the courage to ask a pharmacist for a box of condoms. There were too many people watching me, and they'd know what I was willing to pay for. So I chickened out and went away.

I went wandering through some pink-lit alleys, avoiding the fake kissy winks of insincere whores who'd make their mouths all round like they loved to suck cock in their big lipstick mouths. But I couldn't buy these theatrics. These whores were transparent, and the truth is... I just couldn't get a hard-on.

In fact, I doubted I could even get it up if it came down to it. I'd probably be so petrified that my dick would just hang there like some sort of limp thing. The whore would get mad and I'd be embarrassed. In the end, I'd probably just end up paying her and not getting nothing. And then I'd leave her sexroom and have to look in the mirror for the rest of my life at some loser who couldn't even fuck a whore.

Then I saw a heartbreaking whore. She was older than me, but with the body of a foal. I mean, she was slender, with muscles, and her stomach was long and her thighs were defined. She was dressed in panties as pure as white snow and they went right up the crack of her streamlined ass. I knew I could fuck this whore.

So I approached her and asked how much for a fuck, and she said a number which equaled forty bucks. And I liked her smile — it was warming and soothing, friendly and intelligent. Wow! I was going to fuck this whore all the way to Duluth! I was going to ride her from behind like a pornstar on cocaine! What a cherry piece of nectarine-ass! She was going to eat the pillow! Maybe I'd even fall in love and write a novel about her as well.

But I only had fifteen bucks on hand. So I told her that this was all I had, hoping she'd take that oh-you-poor-poor-boy approach and suck me off instead. It was an unrealistic thought. The next thing I knew, she was closing the door in my face.

At this rate it looked like I was about to turn thirty having never enjoyed the pleasure of a good whorefuck. But I couldn't let this happen. I'd spent too many hours beating my meat to the vision of some fantasy ass. So I followed a stream of hairy fuckmen down a corridor and into a building. I was part of a horny mobius queue taking short quick steps through a darkened labyrinth. And in all the hallways there were girls in the thresholds: Asian girls — some no older than fourteen — who'd reach out and grab me. But still, I couldn't raise my eyes to theirs.

Hell, I thought, I'll just go into one of those nudie booths and watch some stripper rub her crotch against a pole. Yeah, and jerk off. Because that's the kind of guy I am.

So I went inside the porn place where the booth was lit by a dim violet light. There was a low-slung chair in the corner, a box of tissues, and a waste paper basket. The stage was the size of a refrigerator, but separate from me because of the glass.

And there were a whole bunch of buttons aligned on the wall. The instructions, however, were pretty extensive, and since I didn't have the patience to read them, I dropped in some guilders and decided to wing it.

All the buttons had names on them. There was Jaqueline, Myra, Wendy, etc. I punched a button. Nothing happened. I punched another. Again nothing. I dumped in the rest of my money and punched all the buttons. And each time I pressed one, some buzzer would sound in some back room. Pretty soon, all the buttons were lit up. The machine told me I had fifteen credits.

Great, I thought, fifteen credits.

Then suddenly she appeared in the glass: a hot young blonde with a terry-cloth robe on — which was soft and white, unlike her eyes. Which were lasers, burning into mine — as she began to spit syllables at me. First in Dutch, which I didn't understand. Then she tried German. Italian. French. English. She tried five languages and I was amazed.

I mean, here I was some hotshot translator, and I could hardly understand a thing she said. Because I can only understand what's written down — because then I can study it all day long. But she, this Amsterdam stripper — who gets paid for titillating herself — she knows more argot than I'll ever know. She's the expert on language, not me.

"Have you ever done this before!?" she demanded.

"Yeah," I lied, "sure."

She rolled her eyes then brought them back. She could sense my naïveness like a dog smells fear. And then she put her hands on her hips and her robe opened slightly.

"You put the money through the hole..." she began, but I was staring at her tits. They were perfect and pert and firm, like warm fleshmelons. Her robe began to open even more. Now I could see her navel too. Pretty soon I'd be seeing some muff.

"For fifteen guilders I give you a pussy show..." she continued, now speaking with irritation. "For 25 guilders I play with myself. For 35 I fuck myself with a dildo and we come at the same time. So which do you prefer?"

I looked in her eyes. They were blue like mine. She had beautiful blue Teutonic eyes — and that's when her normalness struck me. She could be a student, a teacher, a dental hygienist.

"I put all my money in the machine," I told her. "I don't have any left."

She rolled her eyes again. Now she was really pissed off. So I started arguing about the fact that the money I paid should entitle me to "a pussy show." It was ridiculous. I was arguing with some woman about my right to see her inner-pink. I couldn't believe it.

Anyway, it didn't take long before she became as disgusted with me as I was with myself. And the next thing I knew, she drew her robe taut, tied it, swiveled on one foot, and was gone.

I looked around in the spermbooth. It smelled like dirty semen in there and I was alone. Except for some loser staring back in the glass. It was the kid I once was — turned to scum.

Terrific, I thought, and hotfooted it out of there and back to the train station, where my locker was gaping wide open and all my stuff gone. My bags were gone, my passport was gone, my shitty Zenith laptop was gone, and all the translations I'd ever worked on — gone. Everything Gone!

For a second I thought about maybe being calm about this and maybe even laughing a bit, but I was so wigged out that I decided to go with my initial impulse. I panicked.

"Some Motherfucker Ripped Me Off!" I screamed — then went running to the baggage attendant.

He was speaking with a kindly older couple and I was expected to wait for them to finish their chit-chat. No way! I immediately busted in:

"I Got Ripped Off! Because I'm a loser! A thirty-year-old drug-addict loser who tried to fuck a whore but couldn't even get a pussy show! Because I'm fucked! Understand? Fucked to death!"

The three of them just stared at me.

Then the guy followed me back to my locker while I ranted some more.

"Are you sure it was number 51?" he asked.

"Of course!" I shouted at the stupid idiot. "It says 51 right here on my key! It says it right here!"

I showed him the key. It said 57.

Then I opened number 57 and my stuff was still there.

"Thanks," I told him, and sat down on the bench and shook for a bit. I wanted a drink, I wanted a smoke. But I didn't go gettum. I just sat there instead, gripping my head like a fool.

And twenty minutes later I was on the train and

85

heading off to Eastern Europe. And as it entered a tunnel, I found myself trying not to look out the window — since I knew who'd be there and I didn't feel like meeting his gaze.

CROSSING NEBRASKA AGAIN

This is what happened when I crossed Nebraska and stopped in Columbus to visit Burns Ellison — who's the world's oldest graduate student. Burns is 112.

We went fishing on the North Platte, where it meets with the Loup. There's a spillway there and the place is called "Tail-race." So we were down there drinking beers, waiting for catfish — when this body came floating by.

Well, actually, we couldn't tell it was a body at first. It just looked like some sort of puffed-out thing way out in the current. So we wondered what it was, felt it wasn't right, then went back to fishing — both of us listening to me shooting off my mouth again.

I was telling Burns what Céline said about Genet, according to Kerouac. Which was that Genet would be the only other French writer worth remembering that century. But then Kerouac said Céline dismissed Genet for "obvious reasons."

So Burns and I, we're sitting there and we're fishing and we're wondering what those "obvious reasons" are (because if they're so dang obvious, then why don't we know em?) and then we get down to it:

"Céline," I tell Burns, "wasn't really all that

heterosexual... I mean, in *Death on the Installment Plan* he's breaking out his pecker... and he and some kid are jerking each other off. I think he even jerks off a moron in England."

And Burns laughs at that.

Then alluva sudden another body floats by. This body, however, is yelping "Help... help..."

"Really?" we ask it — because maybe it's just some kid messing around. Because bodies don't really go floating by when you're out fishing with Burns Ellison on the North Platte. Maybe in stories, but not in real life. And this is real life, not no story. So we don't believe her — we can't believe her. And so we ask again: "Really?" — but the head doesn't answer. It just flops its way toward shore.

So Burns goes wading out and offers her an elbow, even though it's only knee-deep. And she takes his elbow and rises from the river. And she weighs at least 300 pounds! No shit.

"Watch out for the fishing lines!" I snap at them.

Then she's standing there — t-shirt all wet, panties all wet, dripping all wet — and she's in shock.

"My daughter's still out there," she tells us.

What a sorry sight you are, I think, looking at her, standing fat with folds, staring down at toes. *Pathetic! Like so many members of the proletariat everywhere... like billions and billions and billions... I mean, look at you... you want sympathy from me? You're just another member of overpopulation... you contribute to the consumption of oil and beef — which is pollution — which is Death! And not only are you dumb enough to get caught in the current, but you're dumb enough to lose your daughter too.*

"My daughter's still out there," she blithers again.

Yeah great, I think, *now our fishing's over, finished,*

ruined, kaput!

I look at her again: baggy, dripping, probably drunk. Ain't my problem, though. I'm gonna fish.

But the next thing I know, a bunch of shirtless local no-necks come kicking down the concrete debris, swinging lanterns, saying "We thought we seen a body go floating by!"

"She lost her daughter," Burns tells them.

"Better Get Billy On The Phone!" one of them yells up the hill. "We Got A Drowning Victim Down Here!"

Then they head off down the Platte, to see if they can find her daughter, snagged in the snags or washed up on shore.

Meanwhile, Burns helps the woman up the hill while I sit there and finish my beer, thinking: *Don't feel much like searching for nobody... too bad for her. Thousands of people die every day... die like bugs... there's too many of us anyway.*

And it surprises me that I can be so cruel, so cold, so unwilling to help when some girl is out there dying right now... that is, if she isn't already dead. But at least it doesn't bother me. I am able to fish on the shore.

Then I figure the cops'll come — and since neither Burns nor I have fishing licenses, I decide we better pack it up. And just in time too. Cuz alluva sudden there are firemen and spotlights and rescue units and dredging boats and even a chopper.

And as I'm reeling in our lines (Burns' specifically) there's a fish on it. It's a big fatty and it's flopping all around. I can't see what it is, though, and then it breaks the line. So Burns and I, we head for the bar.

"Do you wanna be breast-stroking," I ask Burns in the car, "or doing the crawl?"

"I'm sure you'll do me justice," Burns says, "just don't

forget the fish!"

* * * * *

The bartender is a big old mongo crewcut guy with a head shaped like a tree stump who gives me a look when I order two shots of tequila. He stares at me as if I'm out of my mind, then sighs, pours two shots, and brings them over, moving with the speed of an orangutan on anesthesia. He stands above us shaking his head:

"That stuff..." he tells us, then pauses for almost a minute, "... .... it'll kill ya."

But we just laugh and drink our shots. The bartender, though, won't go away. His mouth is open — so we figure he's going to say something. Then finally he says it:

"Last time... I drank that stuff .... I don't know how .... I got...................... .... home."

"Oh," we reply.

He looks away, then back at us, examining us like we're some sorta food he can't understand. Then wiping his brow, he ambles away.

"Boy," Burns says, "he sure gave you a funny look."

"Yeah," I tell Burns, "you're telling me."

The other bartender comes over:

"Hey, hey! Ain't you that Ellison boy?"

"Yeah," Burns says, "Burns Ellison."

They shake hands.

"Hey," the bartender says, "I'm Joey B. I live right across the street from your maw. I used to mow her lawn after you left for college, back in the uhhhhh, 30s."

90

"Yeah, yeah," Burns says, "yeah."

Joey B. is a slick-haired American Pollack, fond of gesturing with his thumb over his shoulder whenever possible. Sometimes twenty times a minute (I actually count). And when Joey B. talks, he leans in real close. Too close.

So Burns and Joey B., they talk about church, they talk about the Army.

"Hey?" Burns asks, referring to the sloth. "Who's that other guy? He sure gave my friend a funny look."

"Oh," Joey B. says, gesturing with his thumb, "that's Jumbo. Jumbo's a good kid."

Joey B. goes away. We look over at Jumbo. Jumbo moves slow in the late summer heat, swatting at flies.

Jumbo is a 50-year-old "kid."

We drink more shots. They only cost 75 cents each.

* * * * *

The next day we go to an earthship. Burns' friends live in an earthship. They built the place out of tires and driftwood. They have a windmill and a gazebo. And out back, there's even a pond stocked full of bluegills.

We drink coffee, eat muffins.

Then, an hour later, I'm back on the road, cutting across the plattelands again. It's a sweltery sweltery hot summer day — a lot hotter than usual — due, of course, to holes in the ozone layer — because we fucked it up.

(which is why there are tornados and hurricanes all over the place — because we let in the winds of space)

Anyway, it's 104 degrees outside and the Grateful Dead are jamming away. Jerry Garcia has just dropped dead, so I decide to cook an octopus tentacle. Yep, I wrap it in tinfoil,

91

pour barbecue sauce all over it, put it on my block, and 40 miles later it's cooked to perfection. I put it in a hot dog bun.

"Tentacle," I tell it, "a whole lotta voices are going down in the next twenty years."

"Cuz this," I tell it, "more than ever before, is gonna be the age of dead rockstars."

The air smells like pigshit.

I drive towards Iowa.

DOGFISH

Grindle, Grinnel, Cypress Trout. Mudfish, Dogfish, Beowulf.
These are bowfin: a prehistoric fish despised on the shores
of rivers and lakes for intercepting bait meant for walleye
and pike. And for the fact that they're "roughfish," which in
Minnesota means it's illegal to return them to the water.

Dogfish are the bastards of the Mississippi.
Supposedly, they destroy habitats. So they're lumped among
carp and suckers in that lowly category of bottom feeders.

Just look at the dogfish: its bullet-shaped head, its
eely long fin, carnivorous jaws, barbels, fangs. No wonder
they're feared. They come from nightmares.

* * *

It's the last blue light of night beneath the U of M
power plant. The fish you catch here aren't good for eating,
but it's a good place to sit and watch the sunset. Upstream,
you can see the downtown skyline, the Dome, the barges, the
sky full of bridges. Downstream, the chromatic museum takes
on dimension — reflecting gold, copper, bronze, silver. It's a
colorful place to wait for a monster.

So that's what I'm doing. And the dogfish beneath me
are swarming in the spillway. Their population is up. I've been

waiting years for this.

I caught my first in Minnehaha Creek when I was a kid, and kept it alive in a ten-gallon tank. For years it hovered there, rippling its fin, until fungus formed on its bone-plated head. Then it died, but it wouldn't go away. I kept seeing dogfish in unlikely places — like along the tracks, miles from the river, all dried up like mummies, or frozen in a stream two feet beneath the ice.

They caught my attention.

* * *

In 1956 the largest recorded dogfish was 24 inches long and 24 years old. But I've seen them longer. And older. And fiercer.

Dogfish are pure muscle. And instinct. And teeth.

And lungs. Or rather, they have lunglike organs. When creeks go dry, they roll themselves in the mud and wait for the floods. Dogfish can breathe air.

But what's more amazing is their madness. Northern pike, catfish, bass — they never get as crazy as dogfish — which can leap six feet in the air and thrash harder and longer than any muskellunge. If you've ever fought a fish in the sky, and then on land, you know you can't just reel in a dogfish. You have to exhaust it.

It's impossible to grip a dogfish. Most fishermen brain them as fast as they can. They know that the lash of a dogfish can knock out a tooth or give somebody a black eye. Seriously, no one can hold a dogfish down.

* * *

But where are their myths?

Sure, there are stories — but none that are written. Even the Chippewa choose not to remember. The *windigo* exists among all northern tribes, but there are no stories of dogfish. Similarly, the Devil has a place in literature, but Isaac Walton and Henry Thoreau never met a dogfish.

In fact, you won't find any records of this fish unless they're scientific. All cultures have rejected them; which is strange, considering that dogfish are from the oldest living fish family on the planet and have been around just as long as sturgeon and gar. Still, their history doesn't exist.

There are no legends of dogfish.

* * *

WHAM! A dogfish strikes my line. And it's the biggest damn dogfish I have ever seen in my life, flopping around like a great silver salmon. I play the drag, pull it toward the bank. POW! It's in the air, it hits the concrete. SLAP! It's back in the river. ZZZZZZ! I beach it on the petroleum sand and climb down the wall.

There's no spot glowing orangely on its tail — which means it's female. And not only that, but there are two fishing lines coming from its mouth as well as a couple trailing from the anus.

This dogfish is more beat than any fish I've ever met. Its underjaw is covered with scarred-up tissue and open-sore abrasions. But then again, all dogfish are lepers.

I gaze down on it and it looks up at me — two creatures regarding each other. And then I do something I never do: I slide a finger under its gill. And it doesn't resist. I heft it up.

What's this? This dogfish defies the description I've just given. She's slack and not even trying to escape. And I can feel her breathing on my wrist — which is such a weird sensation I can't put her down.

(To feel the breath of a fish on your flesh is to realize your connection with it)

I work the hooks out of her mouth, then bite the lines behind. And the dogfish just lies there pretending she's dead.

So I walk her out into the current and place her in the flow. So she can feed and seed and propagate her species. So that all warm waters shall one day swarm with the gnashing jaws of this terrible underdog.

And she rolls belly up. She's lost all her will.

I right the fish and walk her further out. I let her go again, and again a wave rolls her over. This time, though, she fights to stay upright.

And I know she'll continue to fight. Like a battered woman leaving a shelter with no place to go, or a gangkid just released from jail, making his way back to some urban hell, this dogfish will survive.

GITTING ME A GARFISH

"It lies sometimes asleep or motionless on the
surface of the water and may be mistaken for a
log or snag. It is impossible to take it in any other
way than with the seine or a very strong hook; the
prongs of the gig cannot pierce the scales, which
are as hard as flint... They strike fire with steel and
are ball-proof!"

   —C.S. Rafinesque.

"Fishermen from the area of Lake Charles,
Louisiana [say] that alligator gars and American
alligators sometimes fight, with the alligators
usually the victors over their namesakes."

   —Charles Haskins Townsend.

"It has a bad reputation, and there is a difference
of opinion concerning its value."

   —Edward C. Migdalski.

It was those pictures I saw as a kid. Particularly that one of
two guys down in Arkansas with Hawaiian shirts on, posing
beside a ferocious steely alligator gar longer than themselves.
According to the book, their hook was rigged to a piano string

— and according to my imagination, what they used for bait was a whole chicken. So that's why I had to git me a garfish.

Two decades later, I was back in grad school — this time in Louisiana, the garfish capital of the world, where people still fish and bowhunt for gar. And eat them. That is, if they don't despise them for belonging to that ichthyological underclass of scavengers known as trashfish (the enemies of gamefish).

One reason I wanted to git me a garfish was to take a good look at *le poisson armé* (the armored fish), as the French explorers called it back in the 1700s. I wanted to check out that prehistoric alligator head, those razor-sharp fangs, and that serpentine body dating back to the Tertiary days of the Miocene — making garfish (along with coelacanth, bowfin, and sturgeon) one of the oldest living fish families on the planet.

So I asked a tire-repair guy in Lafayette where I could git me a "Cajun barracuda" (as they're sometimes called in Acadiana), and he told me to find Old Henderson Road and drive to where it dead ends at a rotting bridge. The gar swam so thick there, he told me, that I could pick out the biggest one and drop some bait in front of it. He also advised taking a jack handle along for calming them down once I got them up on the bridge.

It didn't take long to find the spot. I went out on the bridge, looked down, and sure enough, there was a skinny snaky garfish swimming on the surface, snapping sideways at bugs, because of its peripheral vision. It was the first wild gar I'd ever seen and it was hungry. So I dropped my worm in front of it, steel leader and everything. The gar bit, I fought it, it got away. And though I went back to that spot at least thirty times, I never saw a gar there again.

But I did get familiar with the Atchafalaya Basin, driving around on the levees, going to bars with six-foot gars mounted on the walls (like the 200-pounder at McGee's) and fishing in the cypress swamps. Where locals told me to use thread instead of hooks, or a piece of nylon wrapped around the bait, so their teeth get tangled in the mesh.

For years, I tried all sorts of methods. And though I saw a lot of gar, I never caught squat except for sunfish.

* * *

The size of gar has been greatly exaggerated. For some reason, the mythical figure of twenty feet is associated with the alligator gar, the largest creature of its species. In *The Angler's Guide to the Fresh Water Sport Fishes of America* (1962), for example, Edward C. Migdalski writes, "Many huge sizes have been recorded by word of mouth; even statements of '20 feet long' or '400 pounds in weight' have been published in past years by reputable scientists." Similarly, *Fishes and Fishing in Louisiana*, published by the Louisiana Department of Conservation in 1933, notes that the "Mississippi Alligator Gar" attains "a length of as much as twenty feet." J.R. Norman, in *A History of Fishes* (1948), then repeats this misinformation, noting that "the Alligator Gar Pike" can reach "a length of twenty feet or more."

Fossil records indicate that millenniums ago garfish got close to fifteen feet. According to Migdalski, though, such behemoths existed on this continent during the last few centuries:

Twelve and 14-foot monsters... lived many years ago in areas such as lower Arkansas, Mississippi, and Louisiana where little or no fishing took place. Undoubtedly, many huge gars were captured and not recorded or shot and allowed to sink... it didn't take long before the real big fellows disappeared from the scene.

The truth, however, is that gar are physically capable of reaching lengths of ten feet if allowed to grow for over sixty years. But reports of such gar are unverified and mostly come from legends. Like the 1818 description by Rafinesque (for whom the shortnosed gar was named), claiming that their "length is from 4 to 10 feet." This figure agrees with the brunt of scientific data, as in "Species Summary for Atractosteus spatula," published on a biology-based museum website, which indicates that the maximum size for gar is "304.8 cm." Still, modern gar hardly ever exceed seven feet, though eight-foot garfish have been reported in Louisiana, Texas, Mississippi, Missouri, Arkansas and Oklahoma during the last century.

There seems to be a dispute about the length of the world-record garfish. According to Migdalski's figures from the 60s, it was nine-foot-nine; but according to the Earthwave Society's 2001 Garsite, it was seven and a half feet long. This same lunker gar is referred to in "Division of Fisheries Facts about Fish in the Southwest" (an article posted on a website of the U.S. Fish and Wildlife Service), where it's reported that the "largest known individual was 10 feet long."

The only consistent thing we know about this gar is its weight. According to most sources, it was 302 pounds.

Nevertheless, there have been reports of heavier gar. According to John James Audubon, a gar "was caught which weighed 400 pounds." Other sources echo this figure, but the facts remain a bit fishy, with hearsay and rumor carrying more weight than official statistics.

* * *

The best evidence of garfish monstrosity comes from photographs. Like the one in *Killers of the Seas*, by Edward R. Ricciuti, showing a bunch of Depression Era men in overalls and hats, smoking cigs on a cobblestoned Little Rock Arkansas street. Beneath the glow of an old time street lamp, a seven-foot gar is strapped to the bumper of a rickety truck. This fish appears to be at least 250 pounds.

Or in the magazine *In-Fisherman*; in an article entitled "Save the Alligator Gar," there's a popular photo from the 30s of a safari-hatted Dr. Drennen cranking back on his rod while his buddy pulls back on a bow, arrowhead poised and ready for release, pointing straight toward the head of a surface-bursting gar. The head of this fish is twice the size of the doctor's.

Next to this picture, an "8-foot 2-inch 210-pound gator gar caught in Red Lake, Hempstead County, Arkansas, 1921" hangs from a tree behind two men with grim expressions on their faces as if the fish deserved it. This lynched gar, with an actual noose around its neck, is gagging at the sky.

Then there's a picture of Barbara Roy and her "unofficial state record garfish" (caught on 20-pound test) hanging beside her. She "caught [this] monster Garfish on her new Zebco 888 rod & reel," according to Cajun Charlie, who sent the picture in to *Louisiana Fishing Magazine*. This gar is two heads higher than Barbara Roy, and she's no midget.

My favorite picture, however, will always be the one in *Fish and Fishing* by Maynard Reece from 1963. This gar weighs well over 200 pounds and is as fat around as a trashcan. It lies in the sand while the fishermen raise its primitive head, showing off its nostrils and fangs. This is the famous photo that first made me ask "What the hell kinda fish is that?"

* * *

On a bayou by Breaux Bridge, a four-foot gar was hooked on a line someone had strung from an overhanging branch. It was flopping all around, just twenty yards away on the opposite bank. I could've swam across, and risked being caught by whoever set that line (an unforgivable offense in Cajun country), but I didn't feel like braving the water-moccasined current. So I just sat there and watched it splash.

Another time, I was out on Alligator Bayou east of Baton Rouge, drinking beer with my buddy Kris Hansen. The water was low and the gar were rolling in the weeds as they do throughout the summer. Kris had a ridiculous oversized lure. It was red and white and looked like a beer can, but every time he cast it out a gar would hit it. He couldn't set the hook, though, because their beaks were too bony for the barbs to catch.

After that, below Plaquemine, one followed my girlfriend's bobber in. We could see it on the surface, its long skinny body tinted gold by the copper water. If I would've had a gun at the time, I would've had me a garfish.

Over by Lake Fardoche, I saw one leap completely out of the water, twist in the sky, then slap down on its side. That gar was longer than most men.

On the levee below Henderson, though, on rutted roads heading into the brush, that's where I'd find piles of dead gar, their bellies slit open, meat scraped out, heads cooked clean by the sun. These were the spoils of garfishermen — who dumped their garheaps by the truckload, sometimes leaving pyramids three to five feet deep.

On one of these roads I discovered a bunch of decapitated garheads. The first was the hugest I had ever seen, taken off a gar measuring at least six feet. The second one was even bigger. But the third one was the biggest bastard of them all! At first I thought it was an alligator skull.

I took it home and threw it on the roof so the sun would dry it out. Meanwhile, I compared the size of this head to the one at Prejean's, a restaurant north of Lafayette. Their trophy gar was six-foot-something and 200-plus pounds. My garhead was almost twice the size of theirs, making it a gar of unspeakable dimensions.

Eventually, I wrapped that garhead up, drove it out to New Mexico, and gave it to my father. He thought it was pretty cool too, so put it on a stump outside the kitchen window. It didn't take long for the coyotes to find it and run off into the foothills with it. Now, somewhere up in the arroyos of the Sangre de Cristos (the land of delicate trout) there's an incredible garhead bleached by the sun, its wolf-like canines grinning at the sky.

* * *

Gitting me a garfish hasn't been easy. I've been down in the swamps for four years now and have pretty much given in to the conviction that it takes someone raised on dirty rice and jambalaya to hook a gar. There are flaws to this argument, of course, since people from all over come to these parts and catch garfish on purpose as well as by accident. Like Japanese tourists going for redfish in the Gulf and hooking pesky gar (because gar can live in saltwater too, like the two six-footers swimming with the sharks at the New Orleans Aquarium).

My point is this: Midwestern fishermen can't catch gar, since it's a different kind of fishing than sitting on the shore and staring at a bobber. Garfishing involves trot lines, traps, and special equipment. But it also involves a tolerance to the heat which Sven and Ollie will never develop, but which Boudreaux and Thibodeaux have become accustomed to. That is, since Southerners have developed a genetic disposition to the heat of the day in the two hottest months of the summer (when gar are most active), they can git out there and git em. But when northerners go out on an August afternoon and it's 117 degrees, they get dizzy from the blazing rays, and after a couple of hours they dehydrate into jerky.

This theory, of course, is not grounded in scientific research. It's founded on fishing frustration, the vast general statement, and the convenience of making stereotypes.

* * *

The fishbooks agree on our lack of information, noting that for the amount of time this fish has been around, we should know way more than we do — especially considering their vast demographics. Garfish once covered an area from Canada down to South America, and only a century ago they covered half the continent. This raises the question of why they weren't observed more, and studied more, in the 1800s. The answer, however, is obvious: Gar are valued less than the common lab rat.

To most eyes that do not wonder at the amazing ganoid structure of their diamond-shaped armor, their fossilific jaws and needle-sharp incisors, the garfish is not a beautiful creature. I once served some garsteaks to Andrei Codrescu, but he refused to eat them, claiming "That fish is just too ugly, man."

This reinforced what I saw as the popular attitude toward garfish, which makes for its stigma in the animal kingdom. Basically, nobody loves a garfish. Therefore, nobody cares — which has affected our knowledge of the species.

As Craig Springer notes in his article "Gearing Up for Alligator Gar":

> It's just ironic... Here we have the second
> largest freshwater fish in the US, and yet
> we know so little about it... The body of
> knowledge on alligator gar is indeed very
> limited. Life history studies are lacking.
> To date, studies on alligator gar have been
> confined to diet, with some cursory inquiries

on the fish's distribution in a few of the states.

Similarly, Migdalski's *Angler's Guide* argues that
our lack of knowledge regarding gar is reflected in their
ambiguous taxonomy: "Authors of technical works on fresh
water fishes state, 'there are fewer than ten species' or 'the gar
family contains about ten species.' This indecisiveness about a
basic fact indicates how little we know about this family."

Within the last three decades, though, biologists and
conservationists, along with government agencies, have been
making efforts to study garfish, since they've pretty much
ceased to exist above the Bible Belt — when half a century
earlier they used to range as far north as the Great Lakes.
Garfish have also disappeared from the West, where water is
less plentiful now.

The majority of garfish authorities are united in
their befuddlement over the great decline in gar populations,
frequently citing "overfishing" as the most likely reason
for their diminishing numbers, while bemoaning the fact
that there's no support for this hypothesis. Since gar
are becoming more and more of a rarity (and therefore a
novelty), "sportfishing" has also been suggested as a cause
for their dwindling populations. Still, there has not yet been a
consensus that garfishing contributes to extinction.

A more compelling argument is that of mass
extermination, which was encouraged by anti-garfish
propaganda from the 30s. For example, government
publications like *Fishes and Fishing in Louisiana* didn't help
the gar's reputation by publishing statements such as this:

> The Gars, so familiar an element in our
> Louisiana fish fauna, are of unusual interest

for many reasons. Numbered among our
most objectionable fishes, they are a pest to
the commercial fisherman and to the angler
alike, for their voracity is responsible for the
destruction of great numbers of useful and
valuable fishes.

Or, as *In-Fisherman* points out, "Historical records verify a
persistent campaign to eradicate alligator gar. As early as
1933, writers called for their destruction... they are a menace
to modern animal life and will wreak vast destruction unless
they themselves are destroyed by game lovers and sportsmen
alike." *A History of Fishes* repeats this sentiment, noting that
"The Alligator Gar Pike... is very destructive to food fishes,
and causes a great deal of damage to the nets of fishermen,
who kill it without mercy. It is not even good eating itself, the
flesh being rank and tough, and unfit even for dogs."

This overall attitude towards garfish, along with
other unstudied accusations and rumors of plague (like the
"parasitic mussel scare," in which gar were falsely demonized
as carriers), eventually led to their classification as trashfish
in close to half the states in America by the middle of the
twentieth century. Up until the 1990s, most states had no
set limit on the taking of garfish. Individual states either
made it illegal to return live gar to the water or they called for
fishermen to destroy them immediately after capture.

A quarter-century of research, however, has revealed
that garfish pose little threat to gamefish populations (ie, bass,
pike, walleye, trout, catfish, etc.). For instance, it used to be
believed that garfish destroy the nesting grounds of other
species to propagate their own. This misinformation has now
been refuted due to recent studies that explain how gar spawn

in warm shallow backwaters, which higher-status fish try to avoid.

Also, as a 1971 study entitled *Food Study of the Bowfin and Gars in Eastern Texas* (published by the Texas Parks and Wildlife Department) discovered, the diet of garfish consists mainly of forage fish — which are defined as shad, bowfin, bullheads, shiners, buffalo, suckers, chubs, carp, gou (sheepshead), gar (yep, they eat their own kind), and other types of "trashfish" generally considered abundant and disposable. This study was conducted at various points from 1963 to 1966, and relied on data extracted from the bellies of bowfin and gar, which share the same diet. Here are some findings collected from February 1, 1964 to January 31, 1965:

> Out of 240 specimens collected, 165 had food in their stomachs. No bugs were discovered, but 23 crustaceans (mostly crawfish) were, along with 302 forage fish. There were 63 unidentified remains, 0 amphibians, 3 instances of detritus (vegetation, sticks, small grains and artificial lures), 4 instances of "unidentified" (meaning completely unknown food items, due to high degrees of digestion), and 13 gamefish.

This means that only 5% of all gar examined had ingested gamefish. No doubt, most of these were sunfish, which are even more common in the diet of gamefish.

Such statistics were found to be consistent with other studies conducted in the 70s and 80s, making it official that the amount of gamefish devoured by gar is minimal. Hence, the argument that gar are destroyers of gamefish has been proven false. And not only that, but it's also been established that garfish play a vital role in controlling roughfish populations.

As individual states like Arkansas looked at their endangered species lists in light of this new information, they began to pass laws to protect garfish. Throughout the 90s, southern states set new limits (sometimes as low as two gar per day), while repealing laws mandating their destruction. Oklahoma started tagging gar in order to track them and understand their habits, while using hatcheries to bring their numbers up. The Tennessee Wildlife Resources Agency even enacted legislation against garfish harvesting, in the interest of developing "constructive management plans that do not regard alligator gar as nuisances to be destroyed, but as beneficial predators that contribute positively to ecosystem stability, the balance among predators and prey, and... exciting angling."

Nevertheless, the experts agree that something beyond overfishing, sportfishing, and encouraging eradication has been a factor in diminishing garfish populations; but they don't know what it is. When garfish researchers come to me, however, I will give them this three-part answer:

1) **Continental Consitpation:** Like salmon, like squawfish, like half the freshwater fish on the planet, garfish can't swim as far upstream as they used to — because of dams. And since dams control flooding, and since there is now less flooding than there used to be, and since garfish migrate upstream, there are now fewer places for gar to spawn.

2) **Delicate Reproduction:** Since garfish spawning is

now pretty much relegated to the marshes and swamps of the South (thanks to the above), flood plains are required where water levels do not fluctuate, so that gar eggs can remain under water for three to nine days in order to hatch. The jettisoning of eggs is a sensitive process, depending on specific plantlife for the fry to attach to after they are born. The fry then need nine undisturbed days to live off their egg sacs before they can leave the spawning grounds. Increased farming and development have been hampering this process.

3) Insecticides, Fertilizers, and Other Poisons: As numerous studies have proven, DDT and other acronyms get into animal fat and are reproduced for generations, softening the outer layers of eggs, causing sterility and lowering the immune system of various species — particularly those at the top of the foodchain. There has been a nationwide ban on DDT for decades now, thanks to conservationist consternation concerning contamination, and infected animal populations have been making a comeback across the country. Tests on gar roe would no doubt yield traces of insecticides and other pollutants, but the lowly garfish is never tested.

* * *

It's frustrating not to git a garfish. Something there is in me that's just gotta git one. My bruised fishing ego is at stake.

That's why I was taking my friend Kevin to the levee again. The day before, we were out there catching minnows to feed to my pet catfish, when we stumbled across a gar spawning spot. The water was high and they were rolling in the grass in the afternoon heat. I had to git me one!

So I waded out with my minnow net and began stalking garfish. They let me get pretty close and I could see them pretty clearly; they were a couple feet long with oblong black spots, swimming in pairs. Must've been fifty or sixty of them.

I'd get as close as I could, but then they'd shoot off. I'd plunge in my net and miss every time. Until I snuck up on a stump, where I could see a couple on the other side, rolling in the weeds. The smart one saw me and shot off, but the dumb one stayed behind. That garfish was a sitting duck.

I positioned the net right above its head, and went for it. SPLASHHH! The garfish shot straight into it. I pulled the net up on the stump and the gar came with it, splashing like crazy. I had it. It was mine. Finally, a garfish!

But then it flopped out of the net and started slapping around on the stump. I dove for it, slipped, and fell into the muck, allowing the garfish to slap back into the bayou.

So that's why we were heading back. This time, though, I was armed with a brand new net from Wal-mart, which I had reinforced and extended with a mop handle.

"Lepisosteus spatula," I told Kevin as I drove, "is known by many names: gar pike, gator gar, diamond-fish, devil-fish, jackfish, garjack, bony pike, billy gar, etcetera."

Kevin didn't seem to be very impressed with my bevy of gar-knowledge. He lit up a cig while I continued:

"Garfish have lung-like organs that breathe air. This allows them to lie in muddy creekbeds, waiting for the rains. Or gulp air on the surface of low-oxygen ponds."

I was an encyclopedia of fascinating gar-facts:

"The roe of garfish is toxic to humans. Certain tribes once made arrowheads from their scales. There's a saying in

111

the Carolinas which goes 'as common as gar-broth.'"

"What do they eat?" Kevin asked, blowing out a plume of smoke.

"Nutria rats," I told him, "ducks, bugs, herons, fish. Some have allegedly eaten soap, as well as giant turkeys, small dogs, and decoys."

"What about humans?"

"There's never been a verified account," I answered, totally prepared for this question, "but there have been reports of gar maulings. The most famous is from 1932, in Mandeville, Louisiana, at the height of American garanoia. A certain Dr. Paine reported that he had patched up a nine-year-old girl who'd been sitting on the edge of Lake Pontchatrain dangling her feet in the water. Apparently, her toes must've looked like teeny weenies, because the next thing she knew a seven-foot gar was dragging her in. She screamed and her thirteen-year-old brother ran to the rescue. He pulled her away and her leg was just a bloody stump."

Suddenly, we were at the spot, ready to git ourselves a garfish. The water, however, was down from the day before, leaving yesterday's eggs exposed to the sun, and the gar were out deeper, rippling on the surface. So I snuck out with my net, just in time to see a gartail rise. It slapped the water and they all shot off.

A fat lotta good all that book-learning did me!

We ended up chasing a bunch of retarded ducks on the shore, trying to get them with my special gar-net. They waddled and quacked while we stumbled after. Kevin went for one and conked it on the head and it went stumbling around like a drunken uncle.

It's a pathetic sight when grown men fail to git a garfish.

* * *

Colonel J.G. Burr of Texas was the Adolf Hitler of garfish. He was the Director of Research of the Game Fish and Oyster Commission in Austin in the 30s, where he tried his damnedest to destroy gar through electrocution, virtually sending thousands to the Chair.

Col. Burr's preferred method of execution was stringing a power line across the bottom of a body of water, then dragging buoys connected to ground wires across the surface. He'd send 400 volts through the power line, and the fish within range would float to the surface, either knocked out or dead.

This shocking behavior on the part of the Colonel was encouraged by various bureaus of research and conservation, which publicly called for inventors "to devise methods for Gar control, since it is clear that this species is a real menace to many forms of fish and other wild life."

Col. Burr went on to construct a special boat meant for the massacre of gars: the Electrical Gar Destroyer. It was an 8 by 16-foot "barge" rigged with a 200-volt generator and an electric net that zapped the fish, then scooped them up. After that, a bright red floodlight hooked up to the bow blinded the gar so the Colonel could brain them.

On the maiden voyage of the Electrical Gar Destroyer, Burr succeeded in wiping out 75 alligator gar and 1000 turtles. After that, he went up and down bayous and canals ridding Texas of garfish (and whatever else happened to be there), even making excursions into saltwater to get gar that had fled the threat of his all-mighty net.

113

Mr. J.G. McGee of New Mexico then took a hint from the Colonel and rigged up something similar in the Pecos River in Roswell. He went to dams where gar had gathered and shocked them to death. Others followed suit, and soon, tons of garfish were floating belly up across the desert Southwest.

Meanwhile, Col. Burr was compiling all sorts of data on killing gar at various depths with various voltages in different degrees of salinity during different months of the summer. He exterminated millions, making a great dent in the American garfish population.

Following a massive gar-kill in Lake Caddo, this is what the great sportsman Col. Burr had to say:

> I saw one immense Gar, which seemed to be
> 7 feet long, spring entirely out of the water
> 30 feet away. His jump was at an angle of 45
> degrees and I am sure he felt the current.
> This jumping of the Gars, whether they went
> into the net or not, produced a thrill which
> can not be found in any other kind of fishing.

* * *

Contrary to claims that garflesh ain't fit for a dog, there doesn't seem to be a shortage of garmeat being sold in the South. I've seen steaks and filets at rinky-dink stores and gas stations all over Louisiana.

In *Fishing Gear Online* there's an article entitled "Gar in the Pan." The author, Keith Sutton, writes:

Actually, gars are rather tasty, a fact that
becomes obvious when you learn of the
hundreds of thousands of pounds of gar
meat being sold each year at Mom-and-Pop
fish markets throughout the country. On a
recent visit to a south Arkansas fish market,
I watched as the proprietor sold hundreds
of pounds of gar meat in three hours, at $3
a pound. Catfish fillets, selling for $2.50
per pound, were hardly touched by the
customers.... "I can't get enough gars to meet
the demand," the proprietor told me. "Once
folks try it and find out how good it really is,
they come back wanting more. The fish are
difficult to dress, but the meat cooks up white
and flaky, and tastes as good as any fish you
ever put in your mouth."

Sutton goes on to tell about how he ate a freshly cut
steak from a 190-pound gar, and how he was impressed with
it. He compares the taste to crappie, before offering up this
poem:

My pan at home it has been greased
For gar he is a tasty beast
I shall invite the local priest
To join me in this garish feast.

Whether the second to the last word in the poem is missing an
"f," I can't say. But I can say what follows in the article: step
by step instructions on how to prepare garfish. Basically, this
is how it's done:

First, cut off the head and tail with an axe, leaving a big long tube of food. Secondly, use tin snips to split the bony hide open, right down the belly. Thirdly, peel the meat back from the armor using gloves to protect your fingers. After that, filet the meat along the backbone, then cut into smaller pieces.

Sutton goes on to list a multitude of recipes, including gar-stew, gar-cakes, stir-fried gar, gar boulettes and garfish Mississippi. So far, this article is the best resource I've found on how to cook gar. It's available on-line at www.outdoorsite. net/fishing/ article_page.cfm?objectid=166.

* * *

After all that gar-study, I couldn't be held back. So I took off for the Gaspergou Bayou Oil and Gas Fields, where it's said the largest ancient gar in the state still seethe beneath the surface — some of them close to a century old. I was armed with a canoe full of milkjugs with guitar strings strung to treble hooks meant for lingcod up in Puget Sound, a bag of rancid turkey necks, two gas cans filled with chum, five cans of dogfood, and my father's 9mm Luger captured off a Nazi soldier.

I also had one bearded Bulgarian with me, Plamen Arnoudov. Last time I took him fishing, he hooked an endangered paddlefish and I beat it to death with a hammer.

We ate shovelnose for a week — which, of course, is illegal in Louisiana.

But then again, so is fishing without a license. Which we intended to do — as almost every single Cajun does. And nobody tells Cajuns not to eat what they catch — that's what they've been doing since the 1600s, hunting and trapping and living off the land. So why should graduate students be any different? Just because the ancestors of Cajuns got abducted from Canada and dumped in a swamp, prompting Longfellow to write some poem about a tree — does that give them more right to fish for free than us? I don't think so.

It didn't really matter, though, because the place we were going was posted "OFF LIMITS." Gaspergou is owned by Texaco, who ran a big old petrochemical processing plant out there on a platform until just a few years ago when the State shut them down. Supposedly, they'd been dumping something that couldn't be mentioned in the papers. Now, however, the platform was abandoned, and that's where we heard the big ones lurked.

So we snuck through the cypresses. For miles and miles, great horned owls stared down at us while egrets nested all around. There were alligators lying on logs and copperheads winding through the duckweed. And when we got to the platform, there were vultures perched on giant pipes overgrown with poison ivy. But from a hundred yards away, we could see the surface rippling.

We stayed where we were, baited up our floats, and tossed them out. The wind was with us, blowing toward the platform. Soon, twenty jugs were making their way toward the gar-swirls, each of them dangling a big honking turkey neck.

Then we broke out the chum. I'd bought a case of slicker (freshwater mullet) at a place called Breaux's in

Henderson (one box, one dollar), then ground them up in the food-processor until it became an oily purée, which I put outside for three days in the sun. When the neighbors complained about the stench, I poured my concoction into the gas cans.

So Plamen and I, we put our spigots on and poured the soup into the swamp. A reeking red puddle began following the jugs, and that's when I saw a long armored back vanish. It was half the size of my canoe!

After that, drifting closer, we made some bait-bombs by pounding holes in the Alpo cans and hurling them out to smolder underwater and get the gar all up in a lather.

We waited. Suddenly a milkjug went under, then reappeared ten feet later. Then another one went down. Then another. The garfish were going nuts over there. We waited until all twenty were bobbing and bopping around the platform. And then we paddled over and pulled one up.

It had a five-foot gar on it, splashing around in a manic frenzy. There was no way we were gonna get it in the boat without tipping over, so I leveled the Luger between its eyes and blasted a hole through its motherfucking head.

Then we saw the incredible. Its pals began attacking it, swarming it, right beneath us. We could see garbacks passing eight feet long, sometimes longer. They were ripping their fallen comrade to shreds and thrashing on the surface, roiling red with blood.

We gripped the canoe and tried to hold on. The buzzards above were screeching like the damned. A couple times the boat almost flipped — and we knew what would happen if we went into the drink. But then the ruckus ceased.

Under the platform, we saw nineteen milkjugs on the run. Something had spooked them. Something that made a tremendous splash, causing us to swivel and see a gar so mongo that I'd lose all credibility as a garfish aficionado if I tried to describe the size of it. I will only say that some of those books weren't so far off, and that its entire chromy backside was cutting across the swamp, coming our way.

The next thing we knew, we were kicking up a rooster tail and paddling like lunatics. Our only thought was to make it to the Spanish moss and get our asses up in those trees. And we did.

And from that moment on, I no longer felt the burning urge to git me a garfish.

TRANSLATING GENET

I once had this idea that a person could do impeccable work in translation without knowing the language. I figured all you had to know was the text being translated, and that's it. The process seemed simple: Look up every single word in a French/English dictionary, do a crappy translation, take it to some French person, have that person tell me my mistakes, then find the better answers. Yeah, I thought, it'd be like doing a crossword puzzle. And since I didn't have the patience to sit through the intensive summer session to satisfy the language requirement for my master's degree, I put my theory to the test.

I'd found some poems by Jean Genet at the University of Colorado Library where I worked as a slacker security guard. They'd been translated before, but what was left of my high-school French was enough to tell me that the English was full of liberties that sacrificed accuracy while supplying the English with more sexual content and flowery language than the French text actually had. For instance, Steven Finch translated "Dont le bel assoupi où s'enroulent les fleurs" as "Whose fair sleepy genitals flowers wrap around," when no genitals were mentioned at all.[1] Similarly, Frank O'Hara and friends added "wombs" where there were none and injected "dear" when Genet never implied it.[2] So I combined my young green rebel ideals about seeking justice for poetry with an independent study.

The French professor I approached was reluctant, especially when he asked me to translate the dedication to Genet's first poem. I told him that "à Maurice Pilorge, assassin de vingt ans" meant "for Maurice Pilorge, twenty-year-old assassin." He rolled his eyeballs, told me the word was "murderer," and then, for some reason I still can't fathom, agreed to work with me.

That was the beginning of a grueling relationship with translating French that I am still involved in, with dynamics that soon became a lot more complicated than I ever expected. But the first two months were great: I spent it on the shore of a man-made lake stocked with tiger muskie. Every day, I'd take my dictionaries there, cast a mud puppy out, translate Genet, then wait for the big one while guessing at tenses I knew nothing about.

Weeks passed and I saw plenty of snakes and eagles and bass, but I never caught a muskellunge. What I did end up with, though, was a rough translation of Genet's 1942 poem "Le Condamné à mort," which freed him from a life sentence in prison. That is, when Jean Cocteau discovered it, he presented the President of France with a petition signed by the Existentialists, demanding the release of Genet on the grounds that "He is Rimbaud." This led Sartre to write *Saint Genet* (1952), which brought instant fame to the homosexual poet-thief.

So I took my translation to the professor, who went through it line by line in exasperation. Ultimately, he gave me an A, but as he told me later, "If you were in my department, I would've failed you."

Wham! I was unemployed and driving around in a gold spray-painted VW van. I found myself up in Seattle, where I went for the bookstores, bought myself a bunch of idiom books, and hunkered down in my grandmother's basement, taking a stab at the next long poem. And going to the library, actually doing research.

But then I lit out again. For over a year I translated on the road, between Colorado, Minnesota, and Seattle, a continuous triangle. For thousands of miles, squinting into verb books and swerving on the shoulder, I wrote on a notebook strapped to my steering wheel. Once a cop pulled me over and shook his head at the books piled up on my dash and the notes taped all over the place. He gave me a ticket for speeding and a lecture on safety, but at least he didn't quiz me on my French.

In the bigger cities I'd hire French tutors to sit down with me and correct my blunders. After a while, I had French friends all over the country who'd help me whenever I rolled into town. Credit cards paid for it all. Back in those days, they grew on trees.

Then I took a tour of special collections. I started up in Canada and drove down to San Diego, stopping at all the major libraries along the way, where there were rare translations of Genet. Not that I was obsessed with Genet (I couldn't connect with his prose), but I was obsessed with seeing how the other translators had handled his strange equations.

That's when I began to form my aesthetics. Retaining the music, I decided, was the most important factor. If Genet used a French word that began with a certain letter, I tried to find an English one that had the same sound. And I didn't believe in keeping to the rhyme scheme, which limited the outcomes and was a tactic I found to be passé. I also tried to avoid using footnotes, since there were publishers encouraging me to find other ways to note multiple meanings, and footnotes can sometimes interrupt the flow. Somehow, I felt this could be done, but I wasn't quite sure how.

Anyway, these were things I was thinking about while winding down an Arizona mountain highway. As usual, I was holding a book in front of my face, glancing from the page to the road to the page to the road (a technique I thought I had perfected), when the next thing I knew I was heading toward a cliff. I hit the brakes, went into a skid. A front wheel went over the edge, and looking down, I saw a valley a mile below me. But releasing the brakes, I shot back onto the shoulder and my momentum carried me into the next curve. I almost lost it ten more times, skidding and releasing, skidding and releasing, until finally I regained control. After that, I vowed only to translate on straightaways — but I didn't always hold to that.

Then one day I got an idea: I'd go to Europe and do the job right. So I sold my van for 600 bucks, packed my bike into a box, and found myself in Amsterdam, smoking hash in Heinekin bars, decoding the poems. I did this for a week, then struck out for France, a hundred pounds of dictionaries strapped to my back. I peddled through the Netherlands and Belgium, but in the Alps of France, a muscle in my shoulder snapped. I didn't care, though. I got on a train and got off in Cannes, the setting of Genet's sixth poem, "Le Pêcheur du Suquet" — where I drank beer on the beach in the glorious burning ecstasy of pain, translating Genet and marveling at all the beautiful breasts. I kept thinking that something was going to happen — but it didn't. I waited, then left.

I had no money, no connections, nothing. I was a fool to be

running around like that — a waste of time, $35,000 in debt. But that didn't stop me. I was mad with romantic translating fever, believing I was part of some story in which I'd go to Paris and things would work out. Because I was determined.

The danger, of course, was that the world was a logical place, and it wasn't kind to illogical kids with naïve ideas about translating languages they didn't know a lick of. Still, I was willing to take that chance. What else was I gonna do? Get a job? Hell no! I was in too deep. So I went to Paris to translate Genet.

I wound up at the English-language bookstore Shakespeare and Company, across the Seine from Nôtre Dame, where I picked up a book about the place and read about its history of putting up expatriate writers like Hemingway and Joyce. Back then, the place was owned by Sylvia Beach, who published *Ulysses* and hung out with the Lost Generation. Until, that is, the illegitimate grandson of Walt Whitman took her store over, then put up Ginsberg, Burroughs, Corso, and others. Even Henry Miller had slept among these books. And supposedly, this tradition of harboring writers was still going on.

I looked around. There were beds in the corners and kids stocking shelves. And then the old guy came in — George Whitman — dressed in a bright maroon corduroy suit, taking giant emu-steps across the room.

"Excuse me," I said. "It says here you let writers stay in your store — "

"NO NO NO!" he shook his head. "You're No Writer! You've Only Been Published In School Publications! You Don't Have The Gumption It Takes!"

I told him I was working on Genet — and suddenly, everything changed. His face lit up, he grabbed me by the arm, and he started parading me through the bookrooms, introducing me as his brand new Writer in Residence.

And that's what I was for the next few years. I lived there rent-free and my only responsibility was to translate Genet for his amusement — sometimes upstairs, but sometimes underground. Where I made myself an office in the catacombs beneath the store, lit the space with candles swiped from cathedrals, and wrote everything by hand.

George fed me. Mostly it was minestrone stew, but sometimes it was meatloaf made with dogfood left over from his gone German shepherd. With all that ketchup, it tasted just like hamburger.

And not only that, I had French friends living in Paris who'd helped me translate back in the states. They brought me food and clothing and were always willing to look over my translations. Plus, there were always plenty of Parisians around whenever I had general questions on the language.

I also got to use the Pompidou Library, the Sorbonne Library, and the Bibliothèque Nationale; but most importantly, the IMEC Archives. Which I went to one day because I'd read that they had the largest collection on "contemporary writers" in all of France (and when the French say "contemporary," what they really mean is "died this century"). But when I walked through the door with holes in my jeans and a tie-dyed t-shirt, I didn't look much like a scholar. And IMEC was for scholars.

The guy who ran the place was Albert Dichy, Genet's chronologist, and a loyal fan of my grandfather's cousin: Herr Dr. Leo Spitzer, a big-time linguist, theorist and literary critic. Monsieur Dichy asked me if we were related, and when I confirmed this, he rolled out the red carpet, brought out the rarest editions of Genet, and introduced me to Edmund White.

Edmund White, the celebrated American essayist and novelist, had just written the book on Genet: a monolithic biography coming out in three different languages all over the planet — but especially in France. Where the Big Genet Conference was coming in the fall — and I was gonna be there!

Yep, Genet was the talk of the town. Along with Proust and Céline, he was now considered one of the three most important prose writers of twentieth-century France. At the newsstands, his face was on all the magazines, and bigshots from all over were coming for the conference. It looked like things were going my way.

Meanwhile, Edmund White filled me in on all sorts of reform-school argot that Genet used in the poems. We discussed what he termed "the secret language of Genet," which had been baffling scholars for more than half a century. There were questions we both had about enigmatic images and instances of plagiarism. Genet had stolen from Ronsard, Mallarmé, Rimbaud, and more. I even told Edmund White a thing or two.

And then, for some reason, he helped me translate the first two poems (and those poems are like twenty pages each). And after that, he gave me the galleys of a soon-to-be-released "filmscript" by Genet (*Le Bagne*), which had a never-before-translated poem in it. So I translated that and added it to my collection. Edmund White then wrote the intro to my book, *The Poetic Voice of Jean Genet.*

By this time I had two publishers, contracts and everything; Mercury House in San Francisco (for America and Canada) and Alyscamps Press in Paris (for Europe and Australia). Plus, I'd begun work on two posthumous plays that had never been seen in English before *(Elle* and *Splendid's)*, which Sun and Moon Press was wild for.

Edmund White, however, warned me that the lady who ran Genet's estate was an "utter bitch" — an assessment I soon agreed with. In 1992 she had sent me a letter telling me that we'd speak about rights when the time came around. But when that time came around, she couldn't be bothered. Basically, my publishers didn't belong to the oldboy club of Faber & Faber or Grove, who had traditionally published Genet in English. It took her six years to tell me this, along with the excuse that Genet (who died in 1986) left specific instructions that his poetry never be published again — in any language. These instructions, however, never stopped her from offering the literary journal *Asylum* permission to publish a Genet translation of mine for £500, or selling Ecco Press the rights to publish Edmund White's version of "Le Pêcheur du Suquet.[3]

Edmund White had always stressed the importance of securing rights before expending energy deciphering, and that might've been good advice for other people, but not for me. I had to have the finished product in my hand, or the lady wouldn't consider it. Besides, I had to know what Genet was saying, even if this meant defaulting on my student loans and flushing years of work down the shitter —so that's why I did it.

In other words, it didn't look like I was gonna get the rights, but that didn't matter. I loved the words and the way they worked together. I also loved being so involved in something that it blurred the world, giving me the illusion that the work I was doing was way more important than eating right and getting sleep and paying off my credit cards.

Six months went by in a flash. I lost track of time. All that mattered was working on Genet. I never took vacations, I always got up early. Because Paris was for work. Serious work.

It got to the point that I hated the poems — from knowing them better than anything else, and for all the time they were taking from my life when I knew I'd never get them published. But still, this hate was a signal that my work was getting tighter, and therefore, closer to completion.

When I'd find myself at two in the morning reworking a line that had been bugging me all day, while all my friends were getting drunk and running around — when I'd work on a poem for two weeks straight, twelve to fifteen hours a day — when I'd gnaw on a chunk of rock-hard bread left over from the day before and have nightmares about trying to keep my footing in a place where the earth kept shaking because that was where I wanted to be and that was what I wanted to do rather than function in society — I understood:

Si vous pouviez me voir sur ma table penché
Le visage défait par ma littérature
Vous sauriez que m'écœure aussi cette aventure
Effrayante d'oser découvrir l'or caché
Sous tant de pourriture.[4]

It meant:

If you could see me leaning over my table
face wasted by my literature
you would know that it sickens me also,
this dreadful adventure
of daring to discover the gold hidden
beneath so much putrification.[5]

I was learning the tricks of Genet: how he'd use a

certain article to mean another; how he'd place a noun five lines from its verb; how "une biche dorée" meant "a buggered youth" — not "a gilded doe" (as previous translators had it). But I was also learning a specialized French. My vocabulary was très Baudelaire. It had to do with death, ships, flowers, the sea. I couldn't speak to people on the street, or understand spoken French, but that was okay. I wasn't there to have conversations. I was there to think in obscure gay prison slang from the 1940s, not get corrected whenever I tried to order a sandwich.

What mattered was sticking to my routine and plodding methodically through the revisions. Granted, learning through mistakes and writing everything by hand was the long hard expensive way of going about it, and an unconventional method barely used by anyone, but it worked for me.

My aesthetics, however, were always in flux. I found that "retaining the music" became just as limiting as trying to hold to the rhyme-scheme or meter. When complex idioms were involved, being faithful to sounds usually led in a false direction. And as I became more and more aware of this, I became more and more certain that accuracy was my main priority.

Still, the accuracy I was shooting for was not a literal accuracy; it was an accuracy that favored conveying the author's intention in American-English, which often changed the elegant tone. Plus, I had to be consistent, and not call attention to awkward moments (intentional or not) in the original works. And there was never one rule for every situation, because every situation had a different set of factors to consider.

I found myself starting to do what I had condemned

other translators for: translating translations, making improvements, and extrapolation. For example, in "Le Condamné à mort," the problematic "Si ma tête roulait/Dans le son du panier avec ta tête blanche" literally means "If my head should roll/in the bran of the basket with your white head" (even though "son," in this highly obscure context, means "sawdust"). So I took translation one step further and translated the phrase as "If my head should roll/in the guillotine basket with your pale head" to convey the author's intention.

Translating sans footnotes was also a challenge, but I held to the belief that it's always possible to allude to multi-meanings in the text. It wasn't as simple as the publishers suggested, and sometimes it took years and years "to discover the gold hidden/beneath so much putrification," but I stuck it out, knowing translation is possible despite the common complaint that it's not. Since translators can get as close as they can, and since that's the most a translation can do, I was confident that the process could succeed if a poet-translator "makes it new," according to the advice of Ezra Pound.

This led to my conclusion that the greatest translating danger there is is the illusion of epiphany. Meaning that when translators believe they're correct about something, because the feeling they're feeling is too strong to be denied (because they've finally come to understand the mindset of a writer), then it's time to step back and allow yourself to be disproved. Or else your work is founded on guesswork.

I also agreed with George Steiner, who wrote that translation is "not a science, but an exact art."[6] It seemed logical to me that a translation could be tested through scientific methodry (in the form of severe scrutiny by multiple authorities). Because the best test of a translation, I figured, was failure.

And since no translation is ever finished (as the Rimbaud translator Louis Varèse once wrote), I failed for a decade. I failed to the point that I proved my theory to myself about not having to be an expert in a language to do impeccable work in translation.

Ultimately, though, the hardest thing I encountered was dealing with the feeling that I owed it to my work to get it published. Which would never happen legally, thanks to the oh-so-generous Estate of Genet, who I dealt with for years through lawyers and agents and publishers. Until finally the lady informed me that if I had any respect for Genet, I'd stop trying to get my translations published.

That's when I resigned myself to the fact that since there was no dealing with her, our impressions of the poems in English would always be based on sloppy translations.

Still, I tried to look at what I learned from Genet as practice for the other French writers I eventually worked on: Céline, Bataille, Cendrars and Rimbaud. But when you labor for ten years on a translating project, "the dreadful adventure" sticks with you. And you can't give up, even when you're forced to.

But I bear no regrets. At least I got to work with the absurdly serious visionary verse and two comic plays, which always held my interest. Bernard Frechtman, on the other hand, translated the highly scatographical prose of Genet's novels of violence and betrayal. And in the end, when he couldn't get his translations published due to a fallout with Genet, he translated himself into an image that exists in almost every single poem by Genet: He hung himself from a tree.

But not me. I put mine on the Internet.[7]

END NOTES

1. *See Treasures of the Night: The Collected Poems of Jean Genet*, Gay Sunshine Press, San Francisco, 1981, p. 63. A literal translation of this line from Genet's 1945 poem "La Galère" (in which "Dont" refers to a splendid strangler and "bel" refers to a cabin boy in the previous line) is "Who the beautiful boy made drowsy, where flowers entwine."

2. See *The Complete Poems of Jean Genet*, edited by David Fisher and Paul Mariah, Manroot, San Francisco, 1981.

3. See "The Fisherman of Suquet," *The Selected Writings of Jean Genet*, edited by Edmund White, Ecco Press, Hopewell, NJ, 1993, pp. 269-75. The year this book was published was the same year that the Estate of Genet agreed to authorize my translation of "Le Condamné à mort." At that time £500 was about $900 — a figure that was unacceptable.

4. From "Marche funèbre," 1945.

5. Quite a few nay-sayers have challenged me on the use of the word "putrification," but it is a legitimate word listed in *The Oxford English Dictionary*.

6. *After Babel: Aspects of Language and Translation*, 3rd ed., Oxford University Press, NY, 1998, p. 311.

7. See www.sptzr.net.

BOB DYLAN'S *TARANTULA*:
AN ARCTIC RESERVE OF UNTAPPED GLIMMERANCE
DISMISSED IN A RATLAND OF CLICHÉS

"Dylan? He's the best living
American poet there is, man!"
—Andrei Codrescu.

For the most part, critics and reviewers have always
stigmatized Bob Dylan as a lousy poet, advising the public
to buy his music instead. When his book *Tarantula* was
published by Macmillan in 1971 the reaction was predictable,
and has been ever since — keeping in league with what is
expected from that failed-artist class bent on bashing the
bards they secretly aspire to be — but can't, for lack of
imagination.

That common thought restated for the millionth
time, I'll take another unpopular stance: I have never felt a
connection with Dylan's music, nor have I ever felt the urge
to worship him like so many fanatics from so many different
generations all over the world. Still, there is something about
him that I feel is worth appreciating.

Growing up in Minnesota, then going to the U of M
(and living under "the watchtower"), I studied the same books

135

Dylan did. I know this because back in those days, at the University Library, you had to sign a slip of paper attached to the back cover whenever you checked out a book. And in the books by the French poet Arthur Rimbaud, the mythic name of Zimmerman was always there, scrawled in the same ink which had underlined passages in French as well as English.

In the meantime, Dylan's most popular songs were being overplayed daily (just as they are today) along with the Beatles on KQ92 — because America loves repetition and rhyming just as much as a parade of clichés. Because the measure of mainstream mediocrity is constantly reflected in the most commercial music of our times; ie, the bubble-gum aesthetics of Britney and the Backstreet Boys, country western, etc.

But back to those whose job it is to maintain the standards of a mass market thriving on lyrical lard: Their jargonistic journalism seeks not literary genius; rather, simple rhythms to secretly pledge allegiance to, since we all go la la la in our heads when we walk down the street denying the silence of our minds. Reviewers rarely being poets and hardly ever scholars, though, it's no surprise that they're out of touch with the most vital voices in the history of verse.

Robert Christgau was the worst. He reamed Dylan out in *The New York Times* when *Tarantula* first came out, stating that the book "is not a literary event because Dylan is not a literary figure."[1] But the thing is, Dylan would be more of a literary figure if Christgau hadn't set the stage for the book's critical reception — which a herd of poetically illiterate reviewers repeated the sentiments of for over thirty years, essentially echoing Christgau's final damning words: "it is a throwback. Buy his records."[2]

Also, the publisher's dismissive introduction (in which

he opted to remain anonymous) didn't help *Tarantula* become recognized as a manifesto of postmodern poetics — which it is. By explaining that the editors "weren't quite sure what to make of the book — except money," then employing the disclaimer "This is Bob Dylan's first book... the way he wrote it,"[3] it's no wonder readers had trouble understanding Dylan's innovation.

Blundering reviewers like Steve Collins then came along and confused Dylan's readership even more by poorly explaining the literary tradition the poetry sprang from:

> *Tarantula* came about after poet Allen Ginsberg urged Dylan to read *Maldoror* by the Comte de Lautreamont (pseudonym of Isodore Lucien Ducasse) and *A Season in Hell* by Arthur Rimbaud, both of them nineteenth-century French surrealist poets and writers. Surrealism is a modern movement in art and literature in which an attempt is made to portray or interpret the workings of the artist's or writer's subconscious mind as manifested in dreams. It is characterized by an irrational, non-contextual arrangement of material. Some describe it as automatic writing, that is when a writer quickly puts his random thoughts on paper without organizing them, allowing interpretation on the basis of the writer's total creative output, whether for a day or a lifetime of effort. Others call it art that is anti-art.[4]

Hence, we now have tons of misinformation informing readers about what Dylan was trying to accomplish. But Rimbaud and Lautréamont were never "nineteenth-century surrealists" — since they predated that movement by half a century (Hey

Collins, look up André Breton and see if he has a manifesto). Plus, Rimbaud and Lautréamont inspired the Symbolists, who in turn inspired the Surrealists, but they never belonged to anyone's club. Also, Surrealism may have been a Modernist movement, but it hasn't been a "modern movement" for over sixty years. One can only conclude that Collins' malarkey about "irrational... arrangement of material" must've come from the same place he got that baloney about a "writer's total creative output" allowing for interpretation.

I am embarrassed for the reviewers of Dylan, who note his poetic influences, but don't have the motivation to look any further. Still, sloppy research is better than no research at all when it comes to trying to understand the purpose of a text. After all, to fully perceive the fine web of meter and music strung throughout *Tarantula*, it takes a "seer" (a term Rimbaud used in defining the voyant: someone who approaches *the impossible* through a systematic *derangement of the senses*), which *Tarantula* accomplishes in conscious dreamlike windings.[5]

Such perspectives on *seeing* are alien to most people who have never studied the visionary goals of Rimbaud, but such lyrical techniques were visible to Dylan — who practiced his own with a skill and ambition rivaling Rimbaud's genius.

The evidence for this, however, isn't in the fact that I say so; it's in the assonance and alliteration which Dylan saw Rimbaud applying to his already super-imagistic verse, making it more musically dimensional than anything preceding it — therefore putting an end to centuries of rhyming in France by slaughtering sonnets, killing quatrains, and foreshadowing the future of free verse.

Dylan, though, didn't just imitate Rimbaud's syllabic acrobatics; he observed how Rimbaud placed similar-sounding syllabes together to create melodic waves — then did it himself in a hauntingly reminiscent way. Note the repetition of the "u" and "a" sounds in the Rimbaud excerpt below, followed by the same sounds in the following Dylan excerpt. Also note the "c" and "g" combinations in Rimbaud, as compared to the "l" and "d" combinations in Dylan:

From "Bottom" by Rimbaud

Je fus, au pied du baldaquin supportant ses bijoux adores et ses chefs-d'œuvre physiques, un gros ours aux gencives violettes et au poil chenu de chagrin, les yeux aux cristaux et aux argents des consoles.[6]

From "Black Nite Crash" by Dylan

aretha in the blues dunes — Pluto with the high crack laugh & rambling aretha — a menace to president as he was jokingly called — go — yea! & the seniority complex disowning you . . . Lear looking in the window dangerous & dragging a mountain.[7]

Language aside, this Dylan passage hardly represents an "irrational... arrangement of material." It is part of a high-art symphony of allegoric metaphor, fertile with commentary on Civil Rights and twentieth-century politics via the ghosts of Kerouac and Shakespeare à la Greek mythology. And any reviewer who can't see this is either ignorant or lazy — like those who fail to notice the same (but less pretentious) intention in Dylan that is automatically glorified in the canonized antics of James Joyce (a "crooner born with sweet wail of evoker, healing music, ay, and heart in hand of Shamrogueshire... googoos of the suckabolly in the rockabeddy... copiosity of wiseableness of the friarlayman in the pulpitbarrel... wideheaded boy!")[8]

Inaccessibility, however, is expected from Joyce; but not Dylan, whose reviewers apparently expect him to condescend to them. Thus, the *Tarantula*'s web is labeled "jibberish," as demonstrated by a recent listing of the "Top Five Unintelligible Sentences From Books Written by Rock Stars" in *Spin Magazine*. Dylan is at the top of the list with "Now's not the time to get silly, so wear your big boots and jump on the garbage clowns."[9]

It's ironic, of course, that those who claim Dylan is unintelligible assume that his words have no meaning, but it's pathetic that they fail to notice who the "garbage clowns" are. If such bumbling media-mongers juggling rubbish took a moment to consider that the poet might be working in a system beyond their comprehension (as Dylan's namesake did), they might decode the metaphor.

Meanwhile, there's an undiscovered continent of sense to be made from the seemingly nonsensical pages of *Tarantula*, which still awaits critical praise for cryptic brilliance. So get past the music, Garbage Clowns, and read the book — but slowly and out loud, pausing with reflection.

END NOTES

1. Christgau, Robert. "Tarantula," *Bob Dylan: A Retrospective*, edited by Craig McGregor, William Morrow & Co., New York, 1972, p. 390.

2. *Ibid.*, p. 394.

3. The Publisher. "Here Lies Tarantula," *Tarantula*, Bantam, New York, 1972, pp. v,vi,viii.

4. Collins, Steve. "Tarantula: Poems," *Book Reviews*, http:// poeticvoices.com/0006BDylan.htm (accessed 2/19/2003), 2000.

5. For more on Rimbaud's visionary aesthetics and *the impossible*, see "Introduction," *The Collected Poems of Georges Bataille*, Dufour Editions, 1998 (2nd ed.), pp. xii-xiii; and Bataille, Georges, "The Malady/Greatness of Rimbaud," *Exquisite Corpse 7*, www.corpse. org/issue_7/critical_ urgencies/batail.htm (accessed 2/21/2003), 2000.

6. Rimbaud, Arthur. "Bottom" (from *Illuminations*), *Œuvres de Arthur Rimbaud*, Mercure de France, Paris, 1952, p. 261.

7. Dylan, Bob. "Black Nite Crash," *Tarantula*, p. 76.

8. Joyce, James. *Finnegans Wake*, Penguin, New York, 1976, p. 472.

9. Compiled by Dave Itzkoff et al. "Top Five Unintelligible Sentences From Books Written by Rock Stars," *Spin*, vol. 19, no. 4, April 2003, p. 86.

RIDING THE UNIT

"on my last day of life on earth
I got to ride a train
and I paid the fare"

—*KH (1964-2003).*

I

Kristofer Salisbury Hansen, always nodding nodding
nodding and rocking on his ass, underneath the overpass,
or in some boxcar — like some totally wired sugar junky
constantly in motion — moving moving moving moving
— then bursting out in a hearty "Markyboy, this is the way
life should be!" adding "Yessirree, yessirree, just two pals, a
twelve-pack, and the open road before us!" while removing a
can of beans from the fire. Then drinking those beers, we'd
tear into those beans and crash out under the starry sky
somewhere in Wisconsin — or out on the golden outskirts
of Fargo — or up in the gloaming twilight of the Rockies
— where huddling over red red embers, brewing coffee in the
bright orange morn, white breath hanging in the air, we'd be
psyched to slide my canoe into the bayou — or lake or bay or

river or stream — then drift with worms, hauling in bluegills, northerns, bass, catfish — Kris in the bow nodding nonstop, a genuine grin on his genuine face, having the greatest time of his life.

I first heard about Kris when I was twenty, at the hospital in Minnie, where I worked in the kitchen, bent on getting drunk on weekends — with the guys, who were always saying "Spitzer, you crazy fuck, you should meet Kris Hansen!" and "If you two assholes ever met, you'd hop some train and never come back!"

But Kris was gone. Because he was mad for trains, obsessed with trains, always talking trains and riding trains and running all over the country on trains — to score some barely legal fishing job out on Puget Sound — or camp out in the scrubby desert working construction — or living in some run-down warehouse on the edge of Gangland USA where he'd get off the BART and run for five blocks, laughing at Crips chasing him with sticks, knives, numchucks, guns.

Which wasn't the way most whiteboys from Edina — the safest suburb in Minnesota — chose to spend their early twenties. Because these were the days of Apple computers, Chevy Citations and Duran Duran — not crashing out in homeless shelters and shivering in sleeping bags. Kris, however, was a fool for adventure — addicted to it, had to have it — so went looking for it and made it happen.

Which is why I was mopping floors in the kitchen he was legend in — and cleaning ovens and going to college while he rushed through the world smoking doobie like the star of his own movie.

And then I heard "He's coming back... he's gonna work here for the summer!" Then "He'll be here next month!" "Next week!" "Tomorrow!" Until there he was, dressed in the

144

same blue uniform as me — nodding nodding nodding — as if constantly agreeing, even when nothing was being said.

I was peeling big purple onions and tossing them into an industrial tub and he was leaning across the stainless steel table, all rosy faced and blond and healthy and gesturing wildly with his broom. He was telling me about picking apples in Washington State with transients like King Tramp and One-Armed Charlie — who got his arm torn off one drunken night trying to catch the hotshot out of Grand Forks, but "Boy could he pick apples!"

Kris was a year older than me with a mischievous gleam in his bright blue eyes. Like me, he was six feet tall, but unlike me, he had a sorta baby face — and was clean cut. So clean cut, in fact, that he actually had an actual crewcut — whereas we all had mullets. Which made me wonder what his deal was. Because nobody had a crewcut in the eighties, and no one hung with winos and vagrants and rode the rails when they didn't have to — cuz that's the action of the past (I kept thinking), that's Kerouac, Rimbaud, danger, madness!

But Kris didn't care. He was bouncing off the walls. "Come on," he said, "we'll go get a six pack, sit up on a railroad bridge and watch the trains come in!"

So that's what we did. And that's when my education began. In riding boxcars, graincars, flatbeds and container freights. In sneaking through the blacknight yards, asking crewmen for directions, always wearing leather boots (and leading with the leg closest to the track when swinging up and into an empty), and never grabbing a train clacking faster than a guy could run.

Kris'd tell me what the workers were doing, where the trains were going, and what they were delivering. If it had four or more units and a bunch of coal cars, it was heading

145

west and crossing the mountains. If it had a bunch of grainers, it would stop in small towns. And if that was the case, Kris'd be like "Come on, we should hop it! Let's do it right now! We'll go around the Great Lakes, come back in a week! What a blast!"

But I always held back. I wasn't quite ready to run off with Kris — who reminded me of Timmy O'Shae, a kid I knew in my trike-riding days, who also had a crewcut. Timmy used to run all over the block and even cross the street, where my parents told me never to venture. And they were right, because one day Timmy drowned in the creek just like that dripping kid on the billboard. It was a "COPS CARE" billboard and the cop was crying and holding a dead crewcut kid.

Nevertheless, I ran with Kris and we checked out the yards, staking out cars. He taught me how to carry a spike to jam into the sliding tracks so the boxcar doors wouldn't slam shut, sealing us in. And he taught me how to pack my bag with a liter of water rolled in the bedroll, and he taught me what to wear and where to step and what to grip and where to look so as not to trip.

And as we yucked and laughed and slapped our knees like a couple dumb kids drunk on the rush of playing vagrants, we saw the seediest sides of the city — where junk gets dumped and couches get burned, where the graffittied concrete of bridges and alleys and tunnels abound, where there are always cardboard camps to be found with barrels and tarps and weathered old men staring out from withered skin — that is, if they weren't passed out by a pile of dogshit steaming next to their heads.

And as the linkages clunked and thunked beneath us, we saw flashing bats, industrial rats, pissed-off punks busting stuff, and snakes and skunks and hawks and possum, and all the woodchucks of the dusk.

And wherever we went, Kris brought the beer. And more times than not, it was Miller Beer — which he'd break out as soon as the hoses hissed, the train jerked, and we took off — so he could raise a toast to all the mangy strays of the night — and smiling nodding laughing clapping, say "Markyboy, it's Miller time!"

II

But we did other stuff as well, particularly fishing. Eighteen years of fishing with Kris — beneath the U of M power plant, or out on some lake an hour from town, or off a spit in the Mississippi where the walleye and catfish were full of PCBs — but we fought them and caught them anyway, surrounded by shining eyes in the brush.

Or we'd shoot pool at some Lake Street dive, or snarf down sliders after bar-time, or crawl around in the closed-down caves of the St. Paul bluffs, where horse-drawn wagons from the 1800s were rotting in the lunar dust. Or drive to some yard in the dead of winter, park beneath a grain elevator, and hike out in the subzero weather with our collars up and our caps pulled down, grab a squat on some worn-out tires, and drink that pisswater beer of his. But on Friday nights, we'd hit the West Bank, especially if Willy and the Bees were playing — because Kris was crazy for that old throaty blues.

And that's the way it went for years: Kris blasting off then coming back. To Minnie. Where finished with the hospital, I was working the parking lots — and it wasn't uncommon to see him pull in in that faded maroon Delta 88 (1966) with reverb on the radio and a totally Bondoed quarter panel. Or maybe he was driving that beat-up Chevy pick-up that didn't have a bed at all, just an open chassis with the gas tank and springs exposed, because his cars were always as crappy as mine.

Then Kris started going to school in Moorhead, where he was getting a degree in social work, growing pineapple plants in five-gallon buckets, raising piranhas, and working with distressed adolescents — who were always lipping off and causing a ruckus, so then he'd have to go in there, tackle some kid, and restrain him till another counselor came to assist him. And when Kris relayed these stories to me, rocking on the balls of his feet in that hyper hyper way of his, it was obvious by the light in his eyes that he got a big kick out of throwing down with juvies.

But he also worked in a homeless shelter across the river, making dinner, setting up beds, and gabbing with the hobos there. Who'd tell him how to avoid the yardcops in Kansas City and how to catch a train to Frisco and what to pack for a ride across Alaska. He got all sorts of stories and advice from them, which he'd use in his travels. And when spring break rolled around, he'd head down to Tijuana or up to British Columbia, then come back all adrenalized, telling tales of the people he met.

Like that kid he met in Mexico and studied Spanish with for years. Or that radical Mormon out in Utah who gave him a ride across Nevada. People he'd keep in contact with, until one day they'd just show up on his doorstep. Because wherever Kris went, he always made friends.

Unlike me, Kris was chatty with strangers and always able to find a connection — whether getting people to give him directions or bullshitting someone with whatever baloney just popped into his head. Like that night we were scoping out some yard from a cliff and started chucking rocks. Someone must've reported us, because suddenly there were spotlights all over us and flashing red lights in the parking lot.

"Come On Out!" a loud speaker blared, so we hid our beers under a bush and came out with our hands up — into a bunch of badges and flashlights in our faces. And in the center of all this: a big thick railroad bull (with a crewcut just like Kris') looking for someone to bust.

"Okay boys, let's see some IDs!"

149

Instantly Kris started smearing it on about how much we just loved trains — because we were fanatics! So zealous were we, in fact, that we belonged to a model train club! We had this model train and that model train and a classic this and a vintage that and we even subscribed to *Model Train Monthly*!

This was news to me, of course, but I didn't interrupt, because Kris was talking them up like some model train nerd who didn't know how to shut the fuck up. Which made a few of the cops smirk at us, but the big thick bull was not amused. He demanded to see our IDs again.

I started reaching into my pocket, but Kris flashed me a glance that told me to stop. Then pulling out his Social Security card, which was totally worn and totally tattered with a chunky brown stain obscuring half the print (because a Sudafed had melted on it), Kris presented it to the cop.

"That's all you have!?" he demanded.

"Yes Sir! You bet!"

The bull pinched it by the corner and took it toward an idling copcar. And when he put his foot down on the bumper to hunker closer and view it in the headlights, his weight forced the front end to descend. And as he stared at the card, Kris started blabbering again, trying to get the other cops to join our geeky railroad club. Until the hulking bull removed his foot, the car shot back up on its shocks, and he returned the card to Kris with a grim look of utter disgust plastered on his ruddy face. We were warned not to trespass again and they let us go.

As Kris told me later, he had a warrant out for an unpaid ticket, so that's why he hadn't handed his driver's license over. Which we laughed about for almost twenty years — Kris guffawing "Did you see how far that car went down when that fat bastard stepped on the bumper? It must've gone down a whole foot!" and me replying "I can't believe how crusty that thing was! He held it like it was covered with shit!" both of us laughing our asses off, rolling on the floor.

III

Kris was always jolly. And jollier than ever with that fleshy cornfed density that had settled in his frame. He loved his beer, he loved his food, but most of all, he loved his friends. Like a bigamist, he was always cruising down to Mankato to hang out with his old pal Miller, or heading to Oakland to powwow with Jerry, or hauling ass to Madison to visit Luther, or who knows, maybe even shooting out to the Yakima Valley to hook up with One-Armed Charlie.

So in the summer of 1989, I got a dirt-green duffel bag like his (since there's only one strap to worry about getting hung up) and we started planning a Fargo run. And that's when the call came in. My roommate's friend, Jeurgen from Berlin, was coming to the USA. I called Kris over in Moorhead and he said "Bring that Kraut up here and we'll take him on a ride he'll never forget!"

It sounded like a plan. So when Juergen arrived, we hopped the Dirty Dog, and five hours later, got off in Fargo. Kris was waiting in the lobby, har-har-harring and grinning like a madman, duffel-bag packed and ready to go.

It was Miller time, though, so we followed him across the street to the Round-Up Lounge (that pucely painted downtown tavern marked by a miniskirted cowgirl twirling a neon lasso), where most of the patrons were homeless alcoholics swaying at the bar and waving to Kris as we walked on in, ordered three flat lukewarm beers, plopped our bags in a cig-butt corner, and started shooting pool.

It didn't take long for some fucked-up Indian with prison tattoos to come over with halitosis and missing teeth. He was saying something like "You think you're better than me! You think I ain't nothing but scum! Well, you don't know who you're fucking with! Gimme twenty bucks!"

He was the kind of guy who wouldn't go away and the tension kept on rising. Until finally he was about to take a swing at Juergen for being Canadian (that's what he thought), so Kris got up on a chair and yelled "Hey Everybody, Check It Out! This Guy Here Is Gonna Assault Us!"

Which worked. The barflies turned their heads our way and the guy paused to consider his next move. But before he could make it, the bartender came over and threw him out.

After that, we guffawed our way all the way to McDonalds, where Juergen ordered "pommes frites" and we doubled up even more. Then someone dropped us off in a field by the tracks and we made our way through the high dry grass.

It was a common run for Kris, going back and forth to Minnie. He knew the times, the trains, and when they started slowing down. So when the freight came along, we hopped a container car and crawled beneath a semi-bed in the wickery North Dakota autumn and started slugging off a jug of Carlo Rossi.

And as soon as we crossed the Red River, the engineers opened her up. Forests began rushing by, the car swayed from side to side, and we drank wine into the dusk — where following a few puffs, this scenario occurred to me: What if you were trapped in a cave and a big old grizzly bear was trying to get inside with its big old grizzly teeth and its big old grizzly breath spraying spittle all over the place and there's nothing you can do but sit there and be petrified as a head the size of a washing machine roars and roars and roars at you and the uvula of death waggles in your face?

And Juergen and Kris were laughing at this. All of us were laughing at this. We were rolling around and holding our

153

sides in our three feet of space, hoods pulled up, winter jackets zipped to our chins, and half a gallon of Carlo left.

By the time we got to St. Cloud we were passed out for good. We didn't even know the train had stopped until we woke up in some yard by the Coon Rapids Dam. It was the middle of the night, totally black, totally cold, and I was paranoid the bulls would nab us — so I ditched my naked lady pipe. We had to hoof three miles to get out of that yard, Kris yakking, Juergen reeling, me stumbling, until finally we found an Amoco station and called a taxi. It cost us twenty bucks to ride into the city, but Juergen was glad to pay, since this had been the ride of his life.

And mine too — up until the greatest trainride ever.

IV

Markyboy——
June 1, 1989
Sun p.m. Oakland CA

You can't imagine the trip I just finished——going through
Oregon along the Mount Shasta Route was up there in the top
3 best freight rides ever... wish <u>you</u> were there to enjoy! I blew a
roll of film so I tossed a couple pictures in. Today's Sunday and
the First Tabernacle Missionary Baptist Church (next door)
is going in full swing and that in itself is an awesome thing!
Oakland is cool as hell! We have some doobie growing (1/2")
+ tomatoes, beans, corn, squash, so this fall will be an "organic
trip" Ha-Ha... Did you score the aquarium? I haven't talked to
my folks for a while. So what's going on here? I scored a Job—
—can you believe that?——Landscaping——oh boy——it's
<u>awesome</u> building decks and shit. We just finished a job on a
rich fuck's house that is literally <u>on</u> the beach——mmmmmm
love that sun and saltwater breeze! No work today, I just
slammed some brews and hung out. I've got my own room here
so I took some scrap lumber that I "conjured up" around the
neighborhood——and built a desk, a night stand, some closet
shelves, and rewired the lighting with a master switch. When I
save a 'lil more cash I'm hoping to score a dimmer for the full
effect. There's a flea market in town where I bought a huge
candle too. Loving life——been recording lots of blues albums.
The record stores out here have tons of older artists so maybe I'll
start a collection of the Delta Blues. <u>I Love the Blues!</u> Jerry's in
a band so it's fun to have the drums and guitars to mess around
with. I'm trying to learn the acoustic, but shit it's a bitch! Back
on the porch there were 3 bikes that were all fucked up so I made

1 out of the 3 and now I can get around town a bit. Nice to save on the subway fare——How's the Scout running? I suppose it's nicer in the warm weather, huh? <u>Cool</u>! The neighborhood here is really fucked! I live on 7th and the gangs control 8th —> 25th, so if I walk that way I'm a dead man. Crack dealers rule the whole place. I was sitting in the park two nights ago and I got robbed——yeah sure——all of 2 bucks. I'm lucky I didn't get knifed in the belly! They were gonna fuck me up and I started running. They chased me a couple blocks. It was dusk and I was over on 9th——oops——learn from those mistakes, right? Did you graduate from the U of M? I know you're taking more classes but I figured you were getting close. I still have two more years of that shit up at Conservacordia. I'd love to hear your thoughts on that malarkey, Ha-Ha. I really love the sheltered environment, no violence, pretty quiet, isolated, and I always get a good night's sleep. Maybe that sounds weird but I'm not a Psycho, I just like the school! Anyways, we'll party in August before I have to boogie up North, O.K.?!! Hit me with a letter.

Love,

Kris

P.S. Possibly Another Train Excursion in August? Let's wait & See....

V

The Greatest Trainride Ever

After spending all night in the Sioux Line Yard waiting for a train that never came, we finally hopped a flatbed in the morning and took it to St. Pauly, where we waited all afternoon for an eastbounder in the shade of a wrecking-yard fence. But then, when it came, we got cut off by an unexpected westbounder, so ended up city-busing it back to the Bridal Veilyard in Minnie — where lounging out by a limestone bridge, we peeled off our shirts and fell asleep in the pungent smell of a rotting carpet somewhere up the nettled slope.

Then it came: an Eau-Claire-bound Chicago Northwestern, clattering below. So we whipped our shirts back on and grabbed our stuff.

It was going fast and picking up speed. Kris was ahead of me. He chose a grainer, flung his duffel into the spot, grabbed the ladder, and swung up after it while I ran to catch up. My bag was bouncing on my shoulder ready to be launched and Kris was reaching out to catch it — but kept glancing forward. And it was a good thing, because suddenly his eyes went wide — due to a big old steel box right in my path, with levers and cranks jutting out all over it.

"Throw!" Kris yelled, so I took the chance. It was a blind hurl straight into the sky, but I didn't have time to see what happened because I was vaulting the thing heroically and Kris was cheering and catching my bag as the train began to get away. And soon it would be going too fast for him to bail. So I made a last-ditch lunge — which was pretty dumb considering what had happened to One-Armed Charlie — but made it.

When I pulled myself up, Kris was laughing hysterically and shaking his bright red sunburned face. He had the twelve-pack out and a beer in each hand.

"Markyboy," he managed to sputter, "it doesn't get any better than this!"

We rattled along for another thirty miles, until the train stopped on the St. Croix Bridge. The smell of creosote was wafting up from the pilings below, where a driftwood logjam had formed.

"Let's grab the crummy," Kris suggested, so we hoofed it toward the Minnesota side. When we came to the caboose, all we had to do was climb the steps and enter it.

It was empty and covered in a film of filth that'd been there twenty years, a spread-eagle woman scrawled on the wall, her wide-open beaver welcoming us as we sat down at a built-in table and began pulling burrs off our socks.

The train took off and we were in Wisconsin, furrowed farmland flashing by — along with cornfields, soy, sod, sunflowers, and every once in a while, a ginseng farm. Then brambled creeks and evergreens and reeded lakes and kids on bikes waiting by the flashing gates for their pennies to get flattened.

And two hours later, we were way above the Chippewa River, crossing an ancient mossy trestle and looking down on the falls below — which would've been spectacular if not for the sewage vats cemented to the cliff walls.

Then cutting through Eau Claire, the train slowed down to yardspeed (10 mph) and moseyed along for a few more miles into the town of Altoona. Where it came to a stop and we hopped off, stashed our bags in some junipers there and strode two blocks to the Rail Rider Inn.

It was a Friday night: Harleys and pick-ups parked

in the street. And entering, the first thing we saw was a sign reading "LEINY TAPPERS 3 FOR $1." So we spent two bucks, picked out our cues, and had such a great time shooting 8-ball beneath the taxidermied bass (black ellipses on their backs) that Kris wrote the brewery as soon as we got back, telling them what a fine time we had in Altoona after riding the train in from Minnie. He gave them my address too, and for the next few years we both kept getting free Leinenkugel t-shirts and bumper stickers in the mail.

After a few games, though (in which Kris ran the table twice), the bartender turned the Skynyrd down and yelled in our direction, "Hey, freight riders! Train's moving out!" But we decided to stay because our train was going on to Milwaukee, where according to some hobos Kris knew, we'd get the shit kicked out of us before we made it out of the yard.

So we went back to our bags, found a spot where the tall grass was matted down and moist deer pellets were scattered all around, and cooked a can of Dinty Moore. That's when Kris taught me not to take the top off the can, but to open it half way and bend the lid back and use it as a handle.

We ended up bivouacking there, but later that night it started to rain. So we packed it up, found another crummy, went on in, and crashed out on the floor — only to be awakened in the morning by the sound of iron banging beneath us.

"Kris," I said, "they're hooking us up."

"It's cool, it's cool," he groggily replied, emerging from his sleeping bag — just as the door burst open and I knew we were busted. But it was just an old brakeman with crow's feet spidering out from his eyes.

"Hey, where you boys going?" he grinned at us.

"Up to Duluth," Kris said.

"You don't want this one," the guy laughed, lighting a cig. "It's splitting up and heading east. Catch the westbound on track 1 round eleven tonight."

Thanking him, we jumped off and the train took off, leaving us with a day to kill. So stashing our bags once again, we took off through a forest full of uniformly planted pines. The needles on the ground had turned a reddish brown and a speckled light was filtering through the canopy above as we emerged on the shore of a pristine lake surrounded by towering granite cliffs and a bright bright turquoise sky. It was like being in a Hamm's commercial.

There was no stopping us. We shed our clothes and dove into the chromy lake, then washed up with a bar of soap, Kris' head nodding on the surface:

"This is it, Markyboy! This is it! This is it!"

And it was.

That evening we had clam chowder and Oscar-Meyer wieners cooked on whittled sticks. There were wild grouse thumping the dusk and field rats rustling in the deadfall behind us. And then at eleven the Union Pacific pulled in to refuel and we grabbed a boxcar on track 1, spiked the door, rolled out our sleeping bags, and had a smoke. And when the train pulled out, its lazy clacking cadence rocked us right to sleep.

We awoke to find the train unfurling in long wide arcs, three units hauling us into the rising sun. We were cruising through a luminous valley, crossing streams, passing pastures, farmers standing on their tractors — until we stopped on the outskirts of a town called Spooner and kicked around in the woods for five hours. But when the brakelines hissed, we were back on and chugging through a redclay rut cut into the earth for miles — past badger holes and sometimes deer, who'd look directly into our eyes as we passed by — because we were mammals just like them.

For hours we snaked our way through the old growth, woodpeckers pecking on naked dead elms, red and gray squirrels scampering around — till we came out on the edge of a birchy marsh and saw a young moose walking gawky.

There were swimming holes with swinging ropes, lilypad ponds thick with algae, dilapidated outhouse ruins, wells gone dry, faded barns with bowing roofs, fences dangling counterweights, rock piles shrouded by wild rhubarb, and brown-eyed susans everywhere.

The train stopped in a hardwood vale, so we waited until another train came from the opposite direction and clacked on by. And when ours departed, we found out why: The double tracks had turned into a single and we were climbing and climbing, winding through the green green green.

Then cresting the ridge, there it was: Lake Superior, vasting out for as far we could see, its distant misted vista merging with the azure as Kris repeated what he said the day before:

"This is it! This is it!"

And again, it was.

We started doing tricks in the boxcar — leaping around, standing on our heads, taking pictures. And as the single track turned back into a double, we drank some beers and ate some salted nutrolls. Until finally the train pulled into the Superior Yard.

Then hitching our way across the long bridge, we made it to the other side: Duluth. Where we followed the tracks to a yard guarded by a chainlink fence, razor wire coiled on top, and every few feet, a sign screaming "STAY THE

HELL OUT!" But the main gate was wide open and no one was there to tell us to get lost.

"It's because of the federal mail," Kris explained, slinking behind a row of tankers, then stepping out and approaching a worker.

"Hi," Kris smiled, "I'm from Fargo. He's from Minnie. Can you point us to a southbounder?"

This guy, however, wasn't so hot to give us directions. He just shrugged and kept on going. So Kris asked another worker, who mumbled something, but nodded toward the farthest track.

Where the boxcars were all sealed up and there was only one rideable car, a grainer right behind the engines. Which we plopped down on and waited on till we felt the first drops of rain.

"This is ridiculous," Kris eventually admitted, "they're gonna see us sitting here, then stop the train and throw us in jail. And if that doesn't happen, we're gonna end up sopping wet. Come on."

Kris jumped down and I followed him toward the front of the train, thinking he was going around it. But when he got to the first huge unit, he slung his duffel over his shoulder and went up the ladder. And a minute later, we were in it.

There were switches and lights all over the place and a small door at the far end, which we opened up and entered. It was a sunken bathroom with a fridge in it filled with tiny plastic bottles full of plastic-tasting water. We closed the door, drank a few, and then heard some guys come in. They were talking to each other and flipping switches. Then they were gone and all we could hear was the downpour pouring down and static on the radio.

But soon we felt the tugs beneath us, so came up from

our hole. The trains was picking up speed. Power poles were flashing by. And suddenly, we were on the US Mailtrain and shooting through the storm at 80 miles per hour, straight back to where we started.

"We're riding the unit, Markyboy!" Kris howled out, eyes lit up and clapping his hands. "This is the best, the very best! We're riding in style, riding in style!"

We sat down in the aisle where we couldn't be seen, took out some salami and cheese, and started making sandwiches. And that's when the alarms went nuts — flashing beeping blaffing blaring like Three Mile Island melting down. To the point I knew we had to bail and I was hustling stuff into my bag, then scrambling for the door.

"Wait, wait!" Kris laughed. "We're going too fast, you'll break your neck!"

Then bootstomps sounded on the unit, the door swung open, a whoosh whooshed in, and a guy blasted in. He took one look at us, barked "What'd Ya Do!?" and started flicking switches.

"Nothing," Kris snapped, "we're just sitting here!"

The guy turned the noises off, then told us "Look, if they see you get off when we pull into the yard, it won't be good for us and it won't be good for you, so we'll slow down coming into Minnie and you guys jump. Okay?"

Kris agreed, the guy left, and we went back to our sandwiches. This time, though, we didn't have to hide, so we sat in the observation seats sticking out over the side and looked out at the drizzling rain, two stories up and rushing toward the Twin Cities.

And two hours later, downtown looming in the distance, a totally corny rainbow came out and the train began to slow. So we went out on the ledge and descended the ladder, bags strapped across our backs, crushed rock rushing below.

"Just wait," Kris said. "They'll slow it down or it's their ass."

Meanwhile, up in the first unit, the engineers were signaling for us to jump. But Kris shook his head, telling me "Nope, not until the brakes start screeching."

Another couple minutes passed and then we heard a grinding sound, followed by a squeal. Kris yelled "Now!" and I dropped my bag and jumped off after it, rolling down the hill stuntman-style. Kris, however, just stepped off, giving them the thumbs up.

Then trekking over to a warehouse yonder, Kris opened the door and marched on in. It was a Hmong sweatshop with a family of workers sewing like crazy — who Kris howdied with slaphappy chatter. They didn't speak a word of English, but he managed to get the message across that we were leaving our bags and coming back later.

Then we were gone. To a mall a mile away. Where we found a bus stop, checked out the times, cleaned up in a public bathroom, got ourselves some Whoppers, bought a twelve-pack, and went back to the sweatshop — where our Hmong buddies were glad to see us. Kris gave them the beer, we cruised on back to the mall, caught our bus, and shot on into the city — Kris nodding like a fiend. Because every molecule in his zipping system was agreeing with every charged particle in mine that we'd just taken the greatest trainride of our lives.

VI

Yo Baby,   *9-24-89*

                                        Fargo

Can't tell you how much yer letter __made my Day__! Holy Shit——
when you said you were hitting Europe, you meant it! What a
__Blast__! Can't wait to hear every minute of it....

   Yes——Yes——Yes——Yes! "Boxcars home——
Sweet——home" is "in there" for middle of October. I get a
mid-sem break——ah——not sure when——possibly Oct 19?
It starts on the Thursday of that week and it goes thru Sunday.
I'll be catching a train home (courtesy BN) and * OH BOY *
would I Love to have you along!!

   __NO FOOLING__, HA-HA!! As for your 'lil idears:

   1) Yeah the fargo farm is "__in there__"——Autumn is just
now kicking in and slowly I'm beginning to notice my life going
by in seasons, not Days. We could explore Autumn '89 "The
early years" Dig?? __Plan on it__!

   2) Hobo Stories: Yeah they're "in there." I did some
interviewing on my journey back from San Fran. Scored
pictures of a couple of 'em. Awesome, Undescribable,
Depressing, Motivating, Earthly, Painful, Lonely, Exciting *are*
a few words that come to mind. (If you want the "real thing," we
can stop in at the homeless hobo shelter where I work Mon, Wed
serving supper/doing dishes. Bring along that old time recorder
of yours and WE'LL play it back when we're 75 and enjoying
a cold one alongside the yard where we got chased away last
summer... O.K.? __Plan ON It__!

   I really missed our correspondence the last month or
two. I guess it's good, though, because it allows for experiences/
changes to share. __Can't wait__!

What's New In My Life:

— School kicking in full steam ahead

— I wear ties on mon, fri just for fun. Chicks Dig Me (just Kidding about the chicks)

— did some mass dating the first two weeks and I Scored a Lover——her name's Lisa and we're really tight. I do everything with her. It actually might crack you up Mark——She's a total purist conservative and I'm trying real hard to "come around" (what, sarcasm?!) anyways we're playing by the Lord's rules (tossed that in just for you).

— haven't had a drop or a puff since the 1st day of class... had a dip of depression and all the chemicals were tossing my reality like a Salad Spinner. My head's clearing out as I write. I'm happier today than ever in my whole Life. Not sure about sobriety goals——maybe thanksgiving.

Currently it's Sunday Morning——took a walk in the clean country wind of Moorhead. I'm sitting on a R.R. bridge over the Red River. When trains come by they go right over my head. It's awesome here.

I really look forward to a long chat. I'll call you in a week and we'll talk Dates/Times for our RR Excursion.

Miss you,

Kristofer

VII

When it came to drinking, Kris was always on and off, sometimes in some halfway house dealing with whatever he was dealing with, sometimes slamming em down right and left. But if he wasn't into having a beer, I didn't need one either, since we always caught a buzz together.

Whatever bummed him out, he never told me. He mentioned chemicals a couple times swirling in his head, but as he also told me, he knew what a drag it was to listen to whiners bitch about their troubles. So he never pushed that stuff on anyone. It was private, something you dealt with by yourself. Something that hit him once in a while, but he obviously had a hold on it. And since he was never bummed out when we hung together, I figured it wasn't serious.

Besides, we were in our mid-twenties and everyone that age gets depressed just from being alive. Plus, it seemed to me he was playing it smart. If Kris had any question about whether he should drink or not, he didn't. So either way it didn't matter. And it was always a blast to be with him, because he was always UP UP UP and yakking away, going "Let's do this! Let's do that! This is the good life!" etcetera.

Back then, though, I didn't know anything about the manic part of being bipolar. I just figured he was whacky in an optimistic way, so I didn't try to make sense of the clues.

Like that day out on Ham Lake, beyond the Greatest Ball of Twine. We were in Kris' aluminum motorboat that he bought from some farmer for $300, me and him and Lisa — who I can only describe as humorless, bovine, and waiting to form an identity, though not really caring if it happened or not.

They were living together in a St. Paul apartment with

a view of the coppery cathedral dome — to the horror of her ultra-religious parents. It was the early 90s, they had both graduated from college, I was back from Poetry School, and we were all having one hell of a time catching sunnies in the white hot heat of noon.

Until I noticed that the stringer beneath us was rising toward the surface and the five or six sunnies on it were trying to keep up with the boat — which was suddenly spinning as we stared at each other with what-the-fuck expressions. Because the water was foaming and churning and whorling like we were caught in some kinda cyclone — and we were. Because suddenly it let us go and we saw it skate across the lake: a small tornado, not much bigger than a house. It'd come right down out of the blue, landed on us, twirled us around, then shot off, zigging as it petered out.

You can imagine how Kris was whooping after that. We got back in his truck, hitched his trailer up, pulled out his boat, and headed off west — Kris nodding that babyfat face and talking about some family he met, some butt-ugly fish he caught, some trip he went on as a kid, how he wanted to weld metal plates all over some junker and make an armored car. He was blasting from subject to subject without pausing, and going further and further away from Minnie — till we were hundreds of miles in the wrong direction. But Kris just kept rambling madly, because that's the kind of guy he was.

Like when he took juvies to the movie, he'd always park in the farthest spot, just to see their jaws drop when they saw they had to walk "THREE WHOLE BLOCKS?" across the lot. Because Kris loved playing jokes — especially while waiting in line. That's when he'd shout out something like "So, did you get that nasty rash cleared up!?" or "Look, stop bugging me to sleep with your sister, you creep!" Once he

168

even sent me a package full of fireworks just to see if it'd make it through the mail, and it did.

So that's who had the wheel and that's who was hauling us out to South Dakota when I had stuff to do in the morning and Lisa was propped up against the door, snoring like a hog.

Anyway, Kris kept laughing, Kris kept yucking, till we were over the border and heading for Wall Drugs, nobody saying nothing — until finally I exploded "Kris! What the fuck are you doing!?"

"Markyboy," Kris shot back, "all you had to do was say the word!" and he stopped the truck, turned it around, and the next thing I knew, we were heading back, Kris nodding to some secret beat only he could hear.

It was the first time I ever wondered if maybe his energy came from something other than the romantic urge to burn burn burn.

VIII

The fishing time that sticks out most in my mind was by the U of M heating plant. Kris and I were fishing with my father and the sun was going down behind the bridge from which John Berryman leapt to his death, as well as plenty others. The lock and dam were just upstream and 35W was rumbling above us — when suddenly I hooked a dogfish that leapt six feet from the froth, twisting its eely armor in the sky and writhing like a dynamo.

Still, I kept the line tight and fought that bitch and fought that bitch while my father and Kris shouted stuff. Until finally I got it along the concrete and Kris climbed down a grate to get it — which wasn't very likely. And this one being over two feet long and packed with solid muscle, my dad and I just shook our heads.

But Kris caught the fish in flight and did as he was trained to do out on Puget Sound with salmon: Placing his hand over its head in what's known as "the bowling-ball grip," he squeezed its eyeballs into its brain.

The fish was instantly paralyzed — enough for Kris to fling it up and into the sky — where we watched it turn and turn and turn and turn — till it came down hard on the asphalt behind us, and jerking quirking spastically, tore off half its scales.

I felt shitty for this fish which we weren't gonna eat — because dogfish taste like crap. All I wanted to do was catch it and let it go, but Kris had just blinded it and screwed it up beyond repair — so I drove my knife into its skull.

Then took it to the taxidermist, who told me that the Governor's son had once brought an eelpout in, but no one had ever brought him a dogfish. He gave me the price of three dollars an inch, then stuffed it and shellacked it and affixed it to a piece of driftwood.

Now that dogfish is on my wall, its mouth flared open just like Kris, staring up in awe of it — turning and turning and turning in the sky — while I watched with my father, wondering why.

IX

And ten years later, we've got beerguts, out on
Alligator Bayou — between Baton Rouge and New Orleans,
where Kris was now a welder. After working with troubled
teens for years, then deciding he would rather labor, he did
a stint in welding school, got a job at a sugar-beet refinery
working up on catwalks, then dropped down to the South,
where I was back in graduate school.

So we were out there in the humidity, the temperature
at least 103, and there were nutria winding all around us,
twelve-foot gators lazing in the sludge, buzzards perched in
the cypresses, and we couldn't get any fish to bite on any
worm.

Until Kris switched to a crankbait the size and shape
of a beer. It was red and white and so honking huge that I told
him no fish would bite on it, but when he cast "the beercan"
out (as we kept calling it), the gars couldn't get enough. The
moment it hit, they'd attack it like they hated it. And each
time that happened, we'd howl and yowl as they slapped the
surface. Beer after beer after beer after beer, they struck like
lightning, but kept getting off.

Finally, though, we gave it up, and drifting there in
the mouth of the bayou, we decided to take a siesta in the sun
with both our bobbers in the water. Until the sound of a motor
woke us from our slumber.

A fluorescent speedboat was coming our way with
a Confederate flag flapping in its wake. It was filled with a
bunch of redneck clowns, all of them holding their beers in
the air as they whipped some drunken waterskier around, who
was also holding a beer in the air. And they didn't give a damn
that we were there. They shot right by us, slicing our lines,

and sending a tide of waves our way, shocking us out of our afternoon haze.

I, of course, was pissed as hell, but Kris was raving "What a riot! That'd be great! Tearing around like that! What a blast!"

And nodding nodding nodding nodding, he swilled his Miller down and raised his empty can to them — loving the Sun, the Swamp, Everything!

Even the fucking idiots.

X

But back to Minnesota, where I knew Kris more than anywhere else, since we were always coming back. It could've been any year, floating down the Snake River, Kris up front, me in the back, beer in the cooler — riffles, rapids, sandbars, branches — but mostly, long slow verdant stretches devoid of other humans — just trees, turtles, vines and ivies — and us, drunk, shouting stuff.

Absurd stuff, violent stuff, sexist stuff, racist stuff — urban stuff of ignorance — dumbshit stuff we never thunk or believed in any way — because it wasn't even us, it was other people — or people we were making up — who were spewing stuff so over-the-top that we were shattering Nature with our nature.

Which is exactly why we did it. Like fucking filthy sailor fucks shooting off their fucking mouths, talking trash to the extreme, we were insulting the living shit out of each other, calling the other the douchiest things we were capable of thinking of — like in our letters to each other, or walking through the supermarket — for the sheer stupid juvenile joy of being assholes to each other.

And so, defecating orally, regurgitating blasphemy, we splattered what we loved most in the world with verbal diarrhea — while catching skinny pike, snagging spinners on the bank, and imagining what the world would hear if the world was there. But the world wasn't there. It was just us feeling the genius of an irony so cruel and ugly that if anyone would've been there, they would've wished a pox upon us.

Which was the point, in a way. Being boys, being blunt. Being ourselves. Being us.

Kris was the funnest friend I ever had. When he'd say

174

"Markyboy, it doesn't get any better than this!" in that cheesy way he knew was cliché, but loved to do anyway, it was so true that I couldn't even see it.

XI

Down in Deep Louisiana, my girlfriend was convinced
that Kris was gay — which I denied, even though it didn't
matter and shouldn't make a difference. I knew he was lonely
living by himself, but Robin saw something else: A guy so
eager to see me that when he came blasting up to Baton
Rouge and sat across the table from us nodding spastic,
she was certain he had something to hide. Like the reason
he wrote me all the time and referred to her as "Blondie"
— which she didn't cotton to at all.

But one night down on Bourbon Street, right
before Kris quit welding in those sweltering hulls where the
temperature rose to 120, we got drunk on hand grenades (a
green concoction made from at least five kinds of booze) and
he confided in me what his deal was — which is nobody's
business but his own.

I'll say this, though: He'd come to terms with who he
was — a friend of many, but intimate with nobody. And I'll also
say this: It's something everybody goes through for a bit, but
with Kris, he couldn't get past it — and it changed him.

And it was the strangest side of Kris I ever saw.
Because as we sat there sucking down the alcohol, he wasn't
slapping his knees or raising any toasts or making any jokes
at all. He was just slumped there, almost still, having revealed
something that was nothing — yet it ate at him like battery
acid and hung there in the air.

We had to get rid of it. So we went to some jazzy
tourist joint where a fat blackman was singing the blues. In
fact, he was billed as the fattest blackman in the world who
had ever sung the blues. And maybe he was.

Meanwhile, two tables over, a Japanese couple was

nodding along with absolutely no rhythm at all. What they did have, though, were giant radiating grins — to be in New Orleans, America, the World!

We decided to send them a hand grenade to push them over the edge, and the guy was so delighted that he sent his little wifey over to bow and bow and bow before us. We couldn't understand a word she said, but her chatter was translatable: They were totally charmed and totally thrilled and in our debt for the rest of their lives. And when we left, he sent her over one more time to genuflect their gratitude.

And a few weeks later, Kris took off for Florida and welded for a while. And the more time he spent in St. Petersburg, the more letters he'd send listing the stuff he'd done alone. Like fishing and hanging out at bars and checking out the shipyards and reading more and more (mostly trainbooks).

But he'd also call me on the phone and tell me how he couldn't stand his co-workers, who were always talking shit about "niggers." And he'd tell me how he missed his sister, and his parents who had moved to Tucson. And how all his friends were forming new lives with wives and children. And how he missed the dirt and fish he knew. But most of all, so I gathered (since he wouldn't say it directly), he missed the sky, the things passing by, and everyone he met along the way.

So when he asked me what I thought he should do, I was surprised. Because Kris never asked anyone this — he always had a plan, a goal, a new place to shoot for.

"Get out," I told him, "go to where you wanna be and quitchyer dang bitching."

Which is exactly what he wanted to hear.

Postcard from St. Petersberg, May 5, 1998 — an arrow over sandy beach drawn in Kris' ink:

> *2 piers. I fished this one several times. Caught*
> *__lots__ of crazy fish. Plus a Bucket Full of Dinner!*

And on the back, pointing to the blurb praising fancy shops on boardwalk:

> *__Lies__! It's a Condo-infested rat race of total*
> *anal ownership closed to the common person*
> *wanting to drink on beach, play reggae, smoke*
> *+ feel rhythm of life Beat.*

Then the rest:

> *Markyboy: Did ya tell Blondie yer breaking it*
> *off yet? Ha-Ha. So happy for you. Hey, I'm*
> *now an official member of the Boilermaker's*
> *Union Local #104 in Washington State.*
> *Thanks for your input on the deal MARK. You*
> *"know" me + I really appreciate your lending*
> *me an ear and tossing in your respected*
> *opinion. So... within the next month I look*
> *forward to seeing you and yours as I pass thru*
> *the Bayou on my continued life adventure*
> **NORTHWEST* to build Ferry Boats or High*
> *Rises!*

Kris loved Seattle with all its trains and planes and cranes and barges. He was always going to Boeing or fishing downtown or checking out the seafood market over at Pike Place.

And since I had family and friends in Seattle, I'd go there every couple years. But when I flew up from Baton Rouge, I never saw much of Kris. Family came first and friends were getting married. I had priorities in Portland and not enough time to hang out on Skid Row. So Kris got placed on the back burner.

Still, I tried to squeeze him in. Like the night we met him at the Blue Moon Tavern. He'd put on some weight, mostly in his face, but was nodding and guffawing like the old days. Because once again it was Miller time — even though he was on the wagon.

But he creeped Robin out for whatever reason and she became more convinced that he was gay. We fought about it. I knew him, she didn't. I was naïve, she wasn't. So when he called all excited to cook us dinner (he'd bought a big old bucket of clams), I felt it would be better to pass.

Then I got my professor job in Missouri, Robin and I got married, and I kept in touch with Kris through email. He was going to computer school, and every day he'd send a one-liner. Mostly it was banter, like "Hey, stop beating your meat and do something useful, Bozo!" Or a geeky "Reformatted my hard drive today. Linux is where it's at!" Or the standard "Watched the westbound come in last night... 4 units picking up timber."

And I'd always respond with another one-liner, then delete his email. Because Kris would always write the next day — sometimes two or three times a day. To the point I'd sigh whenever I opened up my inbox, because his presence there could be counted on just as much as the US Mailtrain bombing down from Duluth.

So I didn't always answer him — my excuse being (to myself) that I was too busy teaching four courses. One of which was a world lit class called Icons of Insanity, in which literary characters were psychoanalyzed with different definitions of "madness." I gave them Freud and Lacan and Gilgamesh and Gogol and we went from megalomania and melancholia to paranoia and addiction, while exploring the question of where one draws the line between obsession and disease. And all the while we were working with these terms, I couldn't even see that Kris was the perfect example of *manic*.

And I should've known. I should've seen in him what I had no trouble seeing in two previous girlfriends diagnosed with the same condition. But I didn't.

Because my vision of depression was too romantic. Because I wanted to believe that there were exceptions — and that Kris had something *über*, which made him *überhuman*. Because, to me, Kris was Rimbaud, creating his own "state of derangement" in order to arrive at poetry in motion. But he was also Neal Cassady blazing his way across the West, "mad to live, mad to talk, mad to be saved, desirous of everything at the same time" (to hijack Jack Kerouac) and never bumming out at all.

As if mood swings can make for myth and trigger art! As if depression wasn't something I'd researched in-depth and had even written a novel about — due to the chaos it caused in my life back in 1996. As if people who keep returning to the same stupid cycles of denial in their lives can just rise above their demons!

Or maybe I was just oblivious. Or maybe I was trying to change what I saw coming. Hell if I know. All I know is that Kris was a friend I thought would always be there.

But I was wrong. Dead wrong.

XIV

Date: 3/30/2002 9:33:42 AM US Mountain Standard Time
From: kristoferhansen@hotmail.com
Subj: ——

Friends & family, please include me in your prayers. These are the facts:

Oct/99
MRI reveals major low-back damage which doctor Puschek does not share with me. 2 doctors ask me if my back pain is work related and I say "no."

April/2000
disabling work injury occurs which I don't immediately share w/ doctor Puschek.

May/2000
MRI reveals new spine damage but films and reports are "lost" with my initial work-injury claim. All remaining MRI films state I am a woman born 1944.

December/2000
Dr. Puschek drops me as a patient in a certified letter.

February/2001
I see 11 different specialists.
Numerous unusual events occur (examples: appointments get cancelled "by telephone" so I show up "unexpectedly" or i wait 1 hour 40 minutes in exam room for a doctor to come in or MRI films get all mixed up, frontal skeleton view disappears or

emergency room visits occur and it is later denied that I was ever there)

March/2001
I have discogram with Dr. Baker, but the MRI films vanish. Aunt Shirley comes to Seattle to nurse me back to health for 4 days. Doc Baker's written report states I need a new disc treatment called "IDET." 1 week later he drops me as a patient, claiming I'm "emotionally unstable"

May/2001
I have high level of anxiety due to pain and confusion. Mom is concerned, flies to Seattle to accompany me to 3 appointments
-1 w/ psychologist Dr. Shelton
-1 w/ Dr. Wright, surgeon who I had seen previously and has a reputation for defending patients
-1 w/ surgeon Kamson.

Mom's Visit=====================================

Mom & I —> appt. w/ Dr. Shelton:
-Shelton tests me for depression using the Beck inventory written exam, tells us I am emotionally stable for surgery, but not "in this system." Refers me to a Dr. Stonecipher 60 miles away in Everett.

July/2001
Mom & I —> appt. w/ Dr. Wright:
-wright refers me to 2 doctors there for a bone fusion consult.

Mom & I —> appt. w/Kamson:

We find out Dr. Kamson can fix my spine without a bone fusion. Says he can't determine treatment needed until he's actually inside my back during the surgery.

Mom returns to
Arizona===================================

May/2001
-Dr. Stonecipher cancels appt. with me w/o explanation
-Dr. Shelton loses written Beck inventory test and changes office notes to reflect no Beck test ever existed.

July/2001
Dr. Yeung does surgery on my spine, but is not authorized to repair the work-related injured disc, but he repairs 2 discs using new technology treatment involving radiation near the spinal cord. The healing time is 9-12 months, with intense pain for several months.

November/2001
My back pain worsens with physical therapy due to irritating the remaining injured disc.

January 2001
Dr. Kamson's nurse asks me to sign a piece of paper allowing him to do whatever work is necessary, and due to psychological reasons, I agree. He did some very painful tests. He told me the MRI revealed 2 problems: one collapsed disc pushing on my spinal cord, which is why I was having pain, AND two, a nerve passage in my low back has blockage due to a large bone vertebra pinching it and it needs to be opened up wider. I have the surgery.

February/2002
My pain meds are increased.

March/2002
I meet a State Judge and tell him my story under oath in the presence of my attorney and the WA Attorney General.
I voluntarily reduce my pain meds by 1/4, but am still having significant burning, stinging, low-back pain.

May/2002
A deposition is scheduled w/ Dr. Yeung and my attorney.
A deposition is scheduled w/ Dr. Kamson and my attorney. We are hoping WA State will settle this dispute without a court hearing. Please include me in your prayers.

love, kris

XV

It weirded me out that Kris was getting religious on me and everyone else on his email list, so I wrote him pronto. But Kris just shrugged the letter off, telling me not to worry, and we resumed our regular correspondence: daily one-liners messing with each other, trying to get each other's goats.

Then in the summer he went to Arizona, stayed with his parents for a while, and had surgery there. I tried to get him to tell me how he was, but he wouldn't give a straight up answer. I pressed him, though, till finally he said he was doing fine.

So I figured Kris was fixed — which is how he seemed when Robin and I saw him over the holidays in Minnie 2002. After picking him up at his sister's place, we drove around the block to Matt's Hamburgers on Cedar Ave., ate Juicy Lucys and joked around, then went out to Lake Nokomis and walked across the snowy ice (Kris refusing to wear a jacket), en route to the Mall of America to check out the Aquarium.

Where Kris was gabbing with everyone in line and nodding away at a million miles per hour. We were going through a transparent tube in a tank full of mammoth catfish, primitive sturgeon, stripy northerns and golden carp, while I stewed about the price. It cost fifteen bucks a piece — money that doesn't matter anymore.

That was the last time I saw Kris. As his father told me later, he collapsed after we dropped him off and was out of commission for the rest of the day.

Once I was back in Missouri, though, and he was back in Seattle, the emails started up again. Then in June I received this:

"We've had some great times together, Markyboy."

"How's your back?" I asked.

He changed the subject. Time went by. Then he sent this one:

"I've been crying for three days straight..."

"Don't bum out," I replied, thinking he was just going through some temporary funk. "I caught a 9 lb. catfish today."

"You're the bestest friend a guy ever had," came the response.

I decided to write back the next time he wrote. But the next day, he wasn't there. Nor the next day. And I'd deleted all his emails, so couldn't send a message to him.

After a couple weeks went by, I knew in my gut that something was up. Maybe he was having another operation. Maybe something worse.

I called Seattle, got his voice mail, asked him to send an email to me — nothing came. I called again. Disconnected. So I wrote a letter and it came back three weeks later. Addressee no longer there.

And I couldn't find his parents and I didn't have his sister's number, so all I could do was check the obituaries. But nothing.

Until one evening two months later when Robin and I were watching a movie. The phone rang, so I let the machine pick it up. It was Kris' father asking me to call him.

I did — pretty much knowing what to expect.

The chronic pain just got to be too much. All he could do was lie there studying computer systems — which wasn't work that came easy to him. But he pushed himself beyond exhaustion and finally the job he wanted got posted. So he pushed himself even harder and made it through the interview. But when it came time for the physical, he couldn't

187

pass it.

And so Kris rode the train down the coast to visit his aunt for the Fourth of July. Then riding back two days later, staring out that Amtrak window, burnt out on the medication and the pain he was ashamed of, and feeling like a loser for being dependent on his parents, he decided that his future was just as fucked as his back.

So when the chemicals came roiling in like the Burlington Northern topping the Continental Divide and flying down the other side, he let the roaring consume him. And there in his apartment, with my dogfish article framed on the wall recounting how he slayed the creature, my friend Kris Hansen built a contraption and drilled it into his ceiling. It was enough to support 200 pounds of pure wasted American boyhood, shot to shit just like that. The rope stretched, his neck cracked — and he hung there like a swinging swinging pendulum finally come to rest.

Made in the USA